Here and at the back of the book are details from some of the drawings featured. Can you find the pages on which they appear?

Also in this series:

LET'S DRAW CATS
dogs and other animals

LET'S DRAW DINOSAURS
pterodactyls and other prehistoric creatures

LET'S DRAW MONSTERS
ghosts, ghouls and demons

LET'S DRAW CARS, TRUCKS AND OTHER VEHICLES

Illustrations by
Darren Bennett, Michael Bentley, James Dallas,
Brian Hewson, Ryozo Kohira, Kathleen McDougall,
Bruce Robertson, Michael Robertson, Graham Rosewarne,
Tim Scrivens, Dino Skeete

© Diagram Visual Information Ltd 1990

First published in Great Britain in 1990
by Simon & Schuster Young Books

This edition published 1993 by
Bloomsbury Books an imprint of
The Godfrey Cave Group
42 Bloomsbury Street, London WC1B 3QJ

ISBN 1 85471 359 0

British Library Cataloguing in Publication data
Robertson, Bruce *1934–*
  Cars, trucks and other vehicles.
  1. Drawings. Techniques
  I. Title
  741.2

Let's draw CARS

trucks and other vehicles

Bruce Robertson

Text by Sue Pinkus

Bloomsbury Books
London

About this book

Cars and trucks are everywhere today. Some people even think there are far too many of them. Getting around in cities is certainly difficult sometimes because of all the traffic jams.

Since their invention, cars have come in all sorts of shapes and sizes, and this makes them great fun to draw. You may think at first that it will be hard to copy a Cadillac or a moon buggy,

---

Pages 8–17

ON THE ROAD

First, in **Part 1**, take a look at some of the very best cars and trucks that have ever been designed. Many have been for family use; but some are sports cars; some are for building work; and others are for the army, police, or for emergency use. (Just a few are called by names that are hard to say if you do not know them. So sometimes we have given you clues to help with this.)

Pages 18–43

GETTING READY TO DRAW

In **Part 2**, find out all you need to know about using pencils, felt-tips, ballpoint pens, brushes, paints and other tools, so that you can then begin drawing cars like a true artist.

---

but this book will show you how easy it actually is to create fabulous sketches that really seem to whiz across the page.

Flip through the pages now, and you'll see how exciting it's going to be making lots of wonderful pictures of cars and other vehicles. There are some great ideas for things to do with your drawings when you have finished them, too.

As you can see, this book has large page numbers. They are there to help you find your way easily to a drawing you might need to look at again while you are working.

Pages 44–61

DRAWING VEHICLES IS AN EASY RIDE!

Part 3 explores the way you can start to draw amazing pictures of cars in step-by-step stages. Begin with just a few basic shapes, and you will soon have pictures of vehicles just like the ones in this chapter.

Pages 62–139

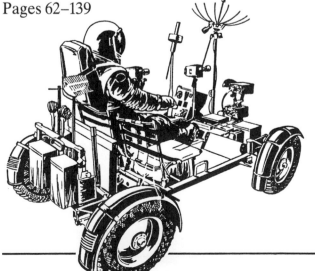

YOUR VEHICLE GALLERY

In **Part 4**, there's a whole range of cars and trucks for you to look at and copy. And there are lots of expert hints and special tips as well. By now you'll be well on the road to making some fantastic drawings!

Part 1

Come car-hunting! This part of the book takes a look at all the different types of vehicles there are and their uses.

This is a picture of a cement mixer. As it travels along, the big drum at the back goes slowly round and round. This keeps the cement inside it from setting into a lumpy mess before it is ready for use. If you would like to draw this truck, turn to page 88 and follow the step-by-step stages shown there.

ON THE ROAD

Vehicles come in an incredible number of different shapes and sizes, depending on their use. Perhaps your family has a car (or even two). It probably only needs to hold a few people and the shopping. But some vehicles have to be large enough to deliver very big pieces of furniture or machinery, to collect all the rubbish from your street, or to transport other vehicles.

Some vehicles carry equipment to put out fires or to save people in an emergency. Others are used to clear snow, to push airplanes, to travel across deserts and rocky terrain or through lakes and rivers. And who knows what the cars of the future will look like? Perhaps they will fly!

Types of vehicle

Here are details from six drawings of six very different types of vehicle. Each has a special use, and has been designed so that it is suitable for this.

See if you can guess which vehicle is which. One is a sports car; another, a military tank. There is also a dump truck used for building work, a fire engine, a family car and an articulated lorry (tractor-trailer).

Now look through the book to find the complete drawings and check if you were right.

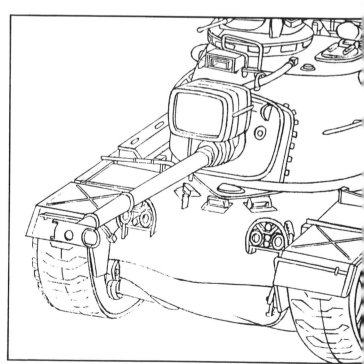

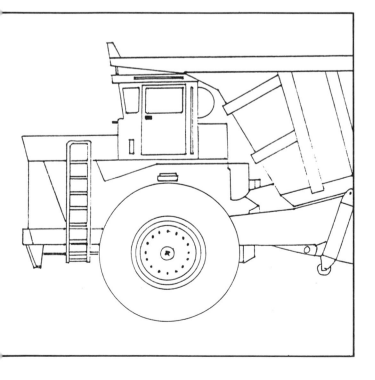

Special vehicles

Whatever the job, there is probably a special vehicle to tackle it. Here are nine types of vehicles. Try to guess the purpose for which each was built. Then check your answers by looking at the bottom of the next page.

1

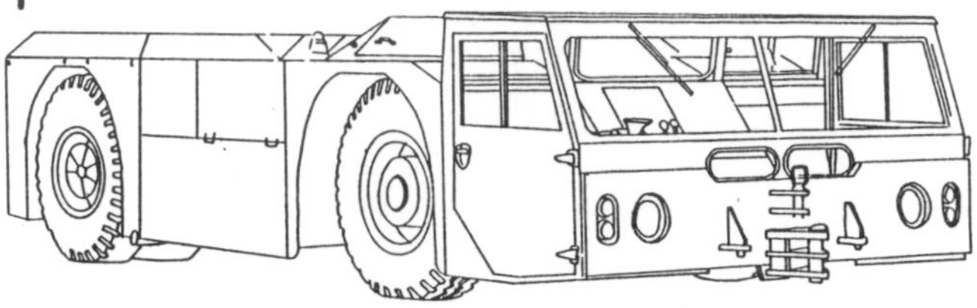

2

3

4

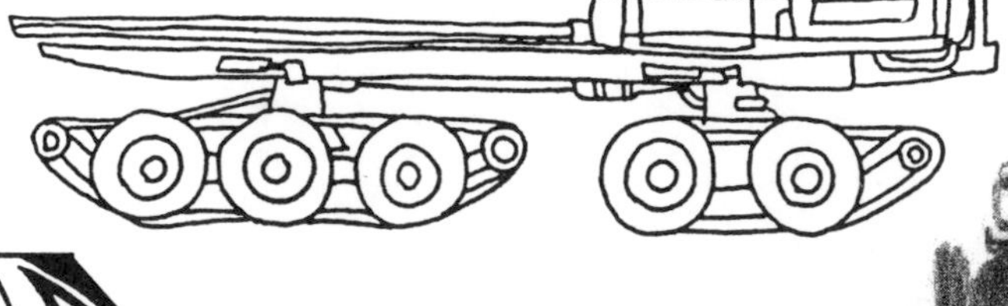

5

GARY GABELICH

REACTION DYNAMICS

THE BLUE FLAME

6

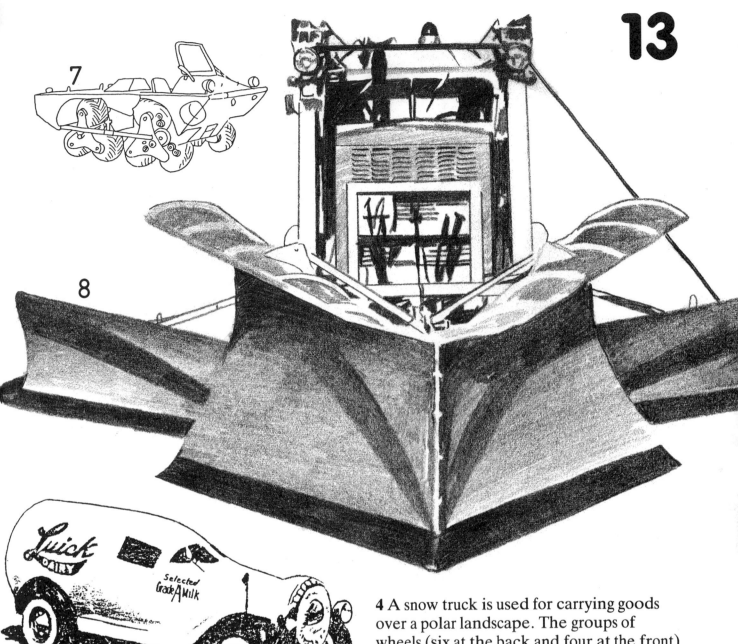

1 This is a heavy tug used to move airplanes around the runways.
2 The circus uses a tow truck like this one to transport animals and also to generate electricity for the circus lights.
3 This car, which looks just like a glider, was built to its owner's special design – just for fun.

4 A snow truck is used for carrying goods over a polar landscape. The groups of wheels (six at the back and four at the front) help it grip in Arctic conditions.
5 This vehicle was built to run on railway tracks as well as roads. (Look at the different wheels it has.)
6 This famous car set a world land-speed record of over 1000 kph (622 mph) in 1970.
7 This amphibian truck is used for water travel and for crossing rocky terrain.
8 This is a snow plough, used to clear roads during winter.
9 An American dairy built this strangely shaped truck many years ago specially to advertise its milk, which it sold in bottles.

©DIAGRAM

Changing styles

You have only to look at the first car in this parade and the last to see how styles in car design have changed during this century. Do you know the names of any of those shown?

1 The 1908 Model T Ford, once the world's most popular car, is very valuable today to collectors. (You don't see many of these on the road now, do you?)

2 This 1920s Ford Tourer had a canvas top which could be folded down so that you could drive with an open roof in fine weather.

3 The 1934 two-door Ford coupé (say *coo-pay*) was a very elegant model.

4 The 1940 Chrysler Traveler was bought by many people for family use.

5 This is a 1950s Hudson Jet-liner four-door car.

6 This 1960s Ford station wagon had wooden side panels for decoration. Why might a station wagon be particularly useful?

7 This 1970s Chevette is a two-door hatchback and part of a move at that time toward smaller cars. Can you think of any advantages of a small car over a large one?

8 The 1980s Peugeot (the French say *Purr-Joe*) 405 is a family car which won a European Car of the Year award.

15

4

5

6

7

8

©DIAGRAM

Built for speed

Sometimes, even if two vehicles have exactly the same function, they do not have the same shape. Here, for example, are 14 different styles of racing car. The numbers on the sides will help you identify them. (Speed is the name of the game, and so every driver is in a crash helmet.)

Numbers 1, 2, 3 and 4 are stock cars and hot rods. These are ordinary cars but their owners have made some special changes to the engines so they will go much faster – up to 322 kph (200 mph) sometimes.

Number 5 is known as a banger. All its glass has been removed for safety. Bangers crash when racing, and the winner is the last car able to move.

Numbers 6, 7 and 8 are autocross cars which race over grass or sand and gravel courses.

Numbers 9 and 10 are midgets and karts, the smallest vehicles to race. Most have an open cockpit where the driver sits.

Number 11 is a hill-climber. These cars do not race each other but try to beat the clock along a course. Each car sets out at a different time, attempting to set a new record.

Number 12 is a slalom racer. The car has to zigzag through obstacles like gates and posts.

Number 13 is an off-road racer which can be driven over very rough country at great speed. (Because off-road racing does not take place on a normal track, drivers have sometimes been known to get lost!)

Number 14 is a drag racer and has an enormously powerful engine that can run at over 604 kph (375 mph).

Part 2

What sort of paper is it best to draw on? How can you use pencils, chalks, crayons and paints to get different effects? And what about drawing with ink?

You'll find the answers to these and many other questions about drawing in this part of the book.

GETTING READY TO   19
DRAW

It is not just important to have the right
paper and tools to make good pictures. You
need to take care over them as you work,
too. So don't rush your drawings. Take
your time.

This is Graham's pencil drawing of a racing
car going at high speed. (You can find out
how to draw it in step-by-step stages on
pages 87.) Pencils are excellent to draw with
and there are several different types. Find
out more about them on pages 24–25.

©DIAGRAM

Good places to draw

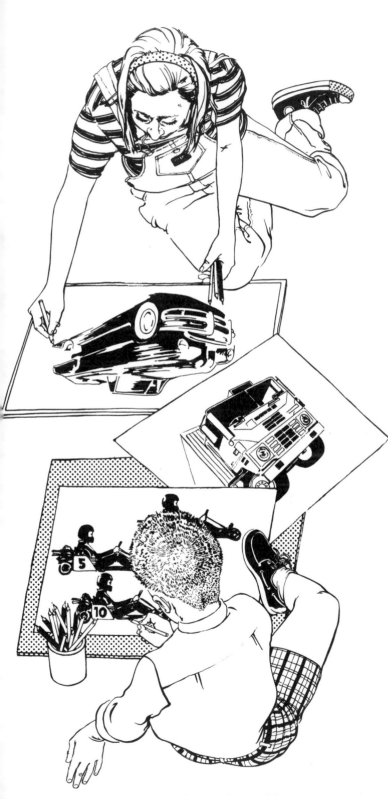

Before you get started, take a little time to sort out the space you are going to work in. Get everything ready, too.

Would you like to spend time drawing with a friend? Or would you prefer to draw on your own? Make up your mind before you begin.

Working on the floor can be fun. It will also give you lots of space so that you can lay out all the pencils, paints, pens and paper you will need. (But make sure that any rug or carpet on the floor is covered with old newspaper or a plastic sheet before you start.) If you work on the floor, you can also stand up from time to time and take a good look at your drawings.

Have a hard surface or a piece of cardboard on which to put the paper you will be drawing on. It will be best, too, if the paper is not so large that you need to lean on it to reach a far corner.

But working on a table is sometimes a bit easier as you can get really close to your drawings when you lean forward.

Whenever you choose to work, make sure you have plenty of light. By a window may be best. If you are right-handed, try to sit so that the light from a window or a lamp comes over your left shoulder. If you are left-handed, try to arrange things so that the light comes over your right shoulder.

Reminders!
- Think about what you would like to draw before you start.

- Decide whether you will use a ballpoint, pencil, felt-tips or paints. Or perhaps ink?

- How large will your drawing be? Plan it so that it will fit the paper.

- Try not to hurry your drawing. You can always come back to it later if someone calls you away.

©DIAGRAM

Which tools for different effects ?

These pictures are taken from three different drawings that appear elsewhere in this book. Can you tell what they were drawn with? Find them in the book to see if you are right. (The pages to turn to are shown by each complete drawing.)

The first picture in each row, going across these two pages, is part of the whole picture at the size it was drawn. The next picture is a detail from it, shown bigger. The third picture shows the whole drawing at a small size. Each has a different effect, doesn't it?

Before you start to draw, think about the sort of effect you would like. Will you need a lot of dark areas? Would you like to be able to rub out any mistakes? Will you want to show a lot of detail? The next few pages tell you whether you should choose pencils, felt-tips, paints or a ballpoint pen once you have decided what you want your final drawing to look like.

On page 77, you will also find some tips for using a ruler and a pair of compasses when you draw, to help with straight lines and circles.

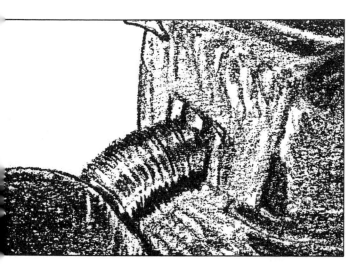

Page 97

Page 61

Page 29

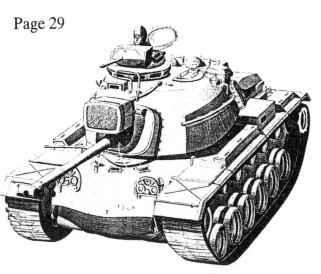

©DIAGRAM

Drawing with pencils

Most people like drawing with pencils. They are easy to use and can be rubbed out when you are planning a picture or if you make a mistake.

When you buy a pencil, you'll see it has a grade (a letter and perhaps a number, too) on the side. If you would like to make dark, smudgy lines, look for grades B or 2B. These are soft. For fine, hard lines, use a pencil with an H or 2H grade.

Remember, too, that a soft pencil will be best for planning a drawing, as a B or 2B pencil is easy to rub out. You can, of course, get pencils in lots of different shades – with red, blue, green, orange, yellow, brown or purple leads, for example.

Pencils work best on paper that has a rough surface. Store them in a box, or keep them in a jar with their points upward.

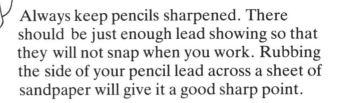

Always keep pencils sharpened. There should be just enough lead showing so that they will not snap when you work. Rubbing the side of your pencil lead across a sheet of sandpaper will give it a good sharp point.

This is a pencil drawing of a Yamaha motorbike racing a Volkswagen Baja Chopper across rocky country. Which do you think will win?

©DIAGRAM

Drawing with pens

Marks made with any sort of ink cannot be rubbed out very easily. This means that, if you decide to draw with ink, you need to do a pencil outline or rough sketch first before you begin your final picture. You can, of course, also trace using ink.

Ink will not give you a chance to shade as you can when you use a pencil. So if you use a pen to do your drawing, you will have to build up darker areas in your picture with lots of dots or criss-cross lines.

Remember to keep the tops on your felt-tips when you are not using them or the ink may dry up.

Try to keep ink off your hands while you are drawing, or you may get blotches and fingermarks all over your pictures. Take care as well not to spill any ink if you are using a fountain pen or dip pen. And try not to get it on your clothes. It is sometimes difficult to wash out.

These three drawings are of a supercharged 1930s Deusenberg, made with a dip pen, felt-tip and ballpoint. Which effect do you prefer? (These cars were very expensive when new all those years ago, and are worth many times more to vintage car collectors today.)

Fountain pens and dip pens

Dip pens – and also fountain pens (which often come with cartridges so you do not need a bottle of ink) – can be bought with nibs of different widths. This means that some will make thinner lines than others when you draw. Many professional artists prefer dip pens. This is because you can change the thickness of a line by using a different amount of ink.

The sort of lines you can make with a fountain pen or a dip pen seem more alive and exciting than those you can make with felt-tips or a ballpoint. Try them all out, if you can, and see the difference for yourself.

dip pen

Ballpoint pens

These tend to smudge, so work carefully. It is difficult to shade large areas with a ballpoint, and you will only get lines of the same thickness. But they are sometimes very useful for tracing an outline.

Felt-tips

These are popular for drawing and come with differently shaped tips. Some make fine lines, and some which are chunky are better for shading. They are also useful for filling in large areas of the background of your picture. (Don't forget to put that top back on!)

ballpoint

felt-tip

© DIAGRAM

Using brushes

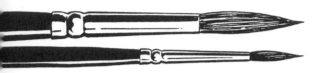

Brushes come in different thicknesses. Larger ones are good for filling in big areas. Finer ones are better for drawing lines. The very best brushes are made from sable or squirrel hair, but cheaper ones can be very good, too.

Use your brushes gently. Don't put too much paint on them or you may get blotches everywhere.

Wash all your brushes after you have used them, and store them in a jar so that the brush ends point upward. This will prevent them from becoming damaged.

This is an ink and brush painting on strong tracing paper, which has been placed over the detailed drawing on page 111.

Use strong paper when you work with a brush. If you paint on very thin paper, your drawing may curl up.

As you paint, start with lighter tones and build them up slowly into darker areas. Wait until large areas are dry. Then add detail with a pen or pencil.

Using paints means you can have a range of tones. Inks are best for strong, dark areas. Look at the different effects produced in these two paintings.

If you use a brush, you can water down your paint or ink to get lighter shades. You can give soft edges to your drawings, too.

This is Mike's painting of a US M48A3 tank. The next two pages show the stages he used, which you can try, too.

©DIAGRAM

Painting a tank

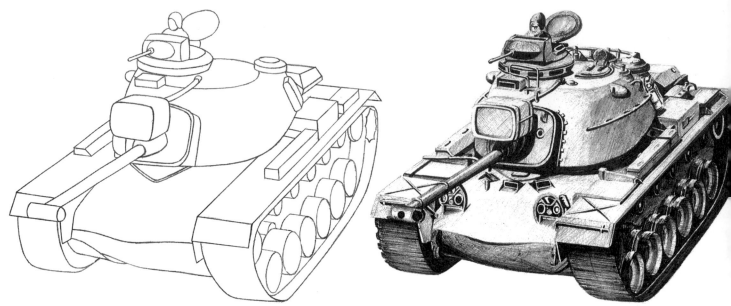

1. You will need a careful outline drawing to help you build up your painting. You can begin by tracing the picture on the previous page (read page 32 if you choose this method). Or you can copy the picture straight onto paper (read page 34 if you choose this method). Or you can construct your drawing using the stages described on page 110.

2. Now place another piece of tracing paper over your outline, and with a soft pencil fill in areas to help you work out which parts will be dark and which will be light. Keep this piece of tracing paper as a guide to help you remember when you come to paint in areas.

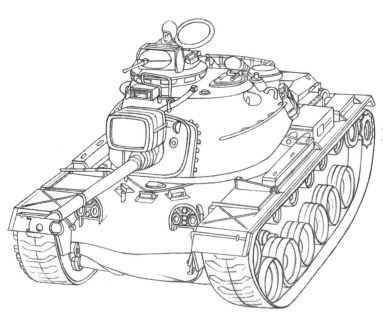

Here is a detailed outline from page 111.

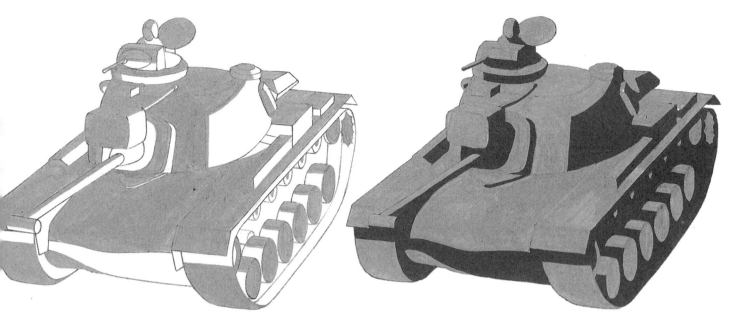

3. Mix your paints so that you have a light shade, and paint in those areas that should be lightest. Keep looking back at that piece of tracing paper and the original picture you are copying.

Now let these areas dry. Be patient! (If you are very bored, perhaps start another drawing while you are waiting.)

4. Mix up a darker tone, and paint in the dark areas. Try not to go over the edges of the light areas, but don't leave white space between them either. Again, let your painting dry.

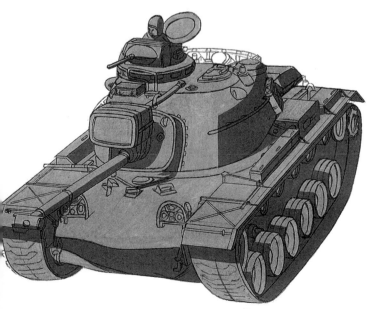

5. Finally, add lots of detail using a sharp pointed soft pencil. You can refer to the picture on page 29 and carefully copy details, or you can place your tracing over the painting and lightly press down positions of some of the objects and details. Go over these marks with either light or dark paint. Tiny details can be pencilled in if this is easier for you.

6. When your painting is finished you could add dark areas of camouflage, just like the picture on page 99.

Tracing

Sometimes it can help to trace an outline of a vehicle from a book. You can then add your own shading.

Choose a picture that has a bold shape so that you do not get muddled over which lines to follow on the tracing paper. A pencil will usually be best for tracing, but you can also use a ballpoint or a felt-tip.

You can trace any picture in this book. To help you start, here is a picture of a dump truck, drawn from the side. It has lots of straight lines to trace, and circles for the wheels, of course.

If you would like to transfer a tracing onto a thick piece of paper or cardboard, you can easily do this using the following method. Try it out on this drawing, which you will also find at a much larger size on pages 132–133.

First cover the picture with clear tracing paper and fix this to the page with the sort of tape that peels off without leaving a mark. This is usually called masking tape. Do not use ordinary sticky tape – it will damage the book.

Using a sharp pencil (grade B), now draw round the main shape. You can also trace any of the details you think it may be hard to copy later, if you like.

Now remove the tracing paper. Turn it over and rub with a soft pencil (again, grade B) onto the lines that show through to the back of the tracing paper. Turn the tracing paper back again to its right side. Now put it on a piece of paper or cardboard. This time, use a hard pencil (grade 2H) with a sharp point and go over all the lines quite firmly but not too hard.

When you take the tracing paper away, you should find you have a shadow of the drawing on the paper or cardboard beneath it. You can use these ghost lines as part of your own drawing.

Remember not to press too hard when you trace as you may spoil the picture you are copying.

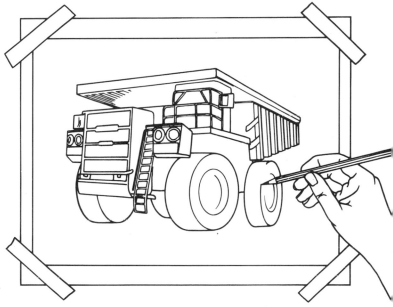

©DIAGRAM

Copying

Copying will give you lots of ideas for your own original pictures. Try hard to get the shapes and tones right, or your copy will not look like the original. Of course, if you use a pencil and the original was drawn in ink, the two will be very different. One drawing will look softer than the other. Here are some useful tips to help you master the art of copying.

Look at the large drawing of a caterpillar-wheeled earth-mover being loaded on to a transporter, shown here. I have started to copy it on the left, as you can see. First of all, I drew in some lines (which I rubbed out later) to remind me that things in the distance always look smaller than those nearer to me. I then sketched the rough outline and marked the position of the wheels.

Then I half-closed my eyes to be sure which parts of the picture should be dark and which light. As I did this and looked at the large drawing, I noticed that almost all the underneath parts are dark but lighter patches appear on the top of surfaces.

Keep checking your drawing
When you are copying, keep looking back at the original drawing to check that you are putting everything in the right place. Check exactly where the wheels are, for example. Do the front ones seem larger than those at the back?

Plan your drawing
Using a soft pencil, draw the basic shape first before you try to copy any detail.

©DIAGRAM

More about copying

This is a car which Jane thinks is super. You can collect pictures of cars and then use them to copy from, which is what Jane has done here – in four different ways.

She made the first drawing by tracing the photograph with a felt-tip, and inked in the dark bits later.

The second drawing was done with a
fine-pointed pen. All the darker areas were
then shaded in with tiny dots. This needed a
lot of care to avoid blotches.

The third drawing is a simple outline in pen.

The last drawing was made in pencil on
rough paper. A lot of attention was given to
the shading of dark areas. Shiny parts were
left white.

©DIAGRAM

Making drawings bigger

It is easy to change the size of your drawing or any picture you are copying from a book by using squares.

First turn the picture you are copying upside down so that the top of the vehicle is at the bottom of the page. This will help you to concentrate when you copy the outline.

Now trace the picture. Next, draw squares over your tracing, as shown, using a ruler for straight lines. Make sure all the lines are the same distance apart. First draw them down your tracing paper and then across the paper.

Now take a larger sheet of paper and again draw squares. But this time make the squares larger than those on the tracing paper. Take care that you draw the same number of squares. If there are 24 squares on your tracing paper, there must be 24 larger squares on the larger piece of paper.

Next, copy the tracing on to the other sheet of paper, matching carefully what is in each square. For example, the third square from the left at the top of the tracing paper should exactly match the third square from the left at the top of your drawing paper.

Watch where the lines of the picture cross each square on the tracing paper. Make them cross at exactly the same points on the larger squares on your drawing paper.

Then turn your paper the right way up. You should have an exact but larger copy of the original outline.

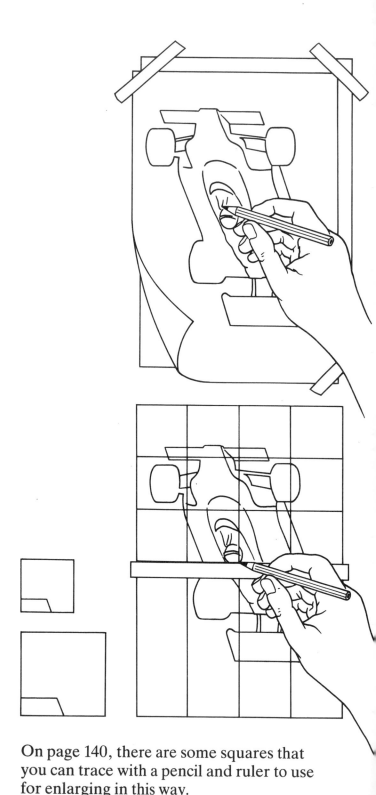

On page 140, there are some squares that you can trace with a pencil and ruler to use for enlarging in this way.

39

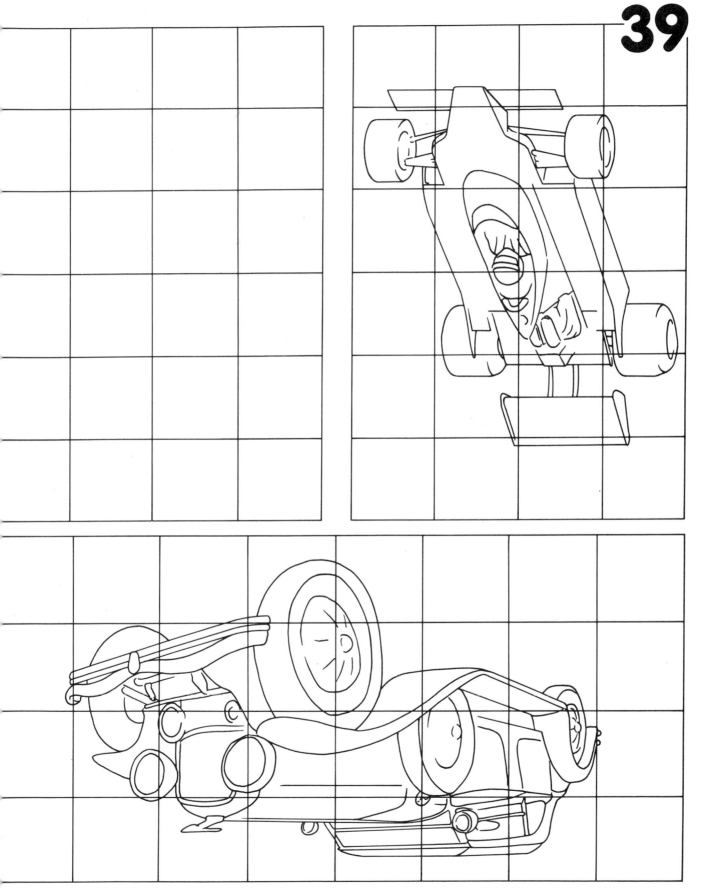

Choosing paper

The sort of paper you should use depends on whether you are working with a pencil, inks or paint. If you use very thin paper, for instance, you cannot work with paints as the paper may curl up.

If you use thick paper, you cannot trace a drawing. But you could transfer a tracing onto the thick paper, using the method on pages 32–33.

Can you find in this book the cars and trucks these children are drawing?

Tracing paper
It is always useful to have some thin paper that you can see through. This will be helpful because you can learn a lot by tracing pictures of cars and other vehicles from books. You can also trace drawings you have already made.

Looking after your paper
A lot of people throw away good paper that you might use for drawing. If someone in your family does this, see if you can rescue it. Even small pieces are useful for rough sketches. Save them until the next time you draw.

Keep all your drawing paper flat. But if it comes in a roll, simply roll it back the other way to stop it from curling up again.

Always work with clean hands. This will help you avoid horrid fingermarks all over your work.

Points to remember about paper
- Tracing paper is very useful if you want to copy drawings from books. You can also use it to transfer drawings onto cardboard or thick paper. But you cannot use a paintbrush on tracing paper very well.
- Smooth paper is usually good for felt-tips and soft pencils. But it is not very strong, so it is best not to use water-paints on this sort of paper.
- Some papers, which you can buy in an art shop and come in lots of different shades other than white, and will usually take paint.
- Strong drawing paper is also sold in art shops and will usually have a rough surface. This means it is good for pencils, inks and paints.
- The thickness of a paper is called its weight. So when you buy paper, you can ask for a heavyweight or lightweight sort.

Drawing pads
You can buy paper in single sheets at an art shop. But you can also buy drawing pads. These are often a good idea as it means you can keep all your pictures together in one place. You could also label a drawing pad on the front cover with the title *My Car and Truck Sketchbook* and add your name.

©DIAGRAM

Using your drawings

There are lots of interesting things you can do with your drawings of vehicles when you have finished them. So try to think about how you would like to use your pictures before you start. Here are some ideas.

Try cutting out simple car shapes and making them into mobiles to hang up with a thread or some wire from the ceiling. It will be best to draw on cardboard rather than paper for this. Get an adult to help you put up the mobile.

You can make a frieze by drawing rows of different cars along a roll of paper, then put it up on the wall of your room.

You could also make a stencil to help you make patterns all along your frieze by cutting out the shape of a vehicle on a smaller piece of paper. Fasten this piece of paper to your roll of paper with masking tape, and then fill in the cut-out shape with paint. Remove the piece of paper when the

paint is dry, and use it again a little way along the roll.

Perhaps keep a scrapbook and put all your drawings in it as well as any pictures of cars that you cut out from newspapers and magazines, and postcards if you have some. You could even make your own magazines about different vehicles which your friends and family might enjoy reading. Give them names like *Car Weekly* or *Motoring Fun*.

You can also make very detailed drawings of vehicles to display on the wall as posters. Sign your drawings when you have finished them, either with your initials or your whole name in one corner. Perhaps put the date, too. If they are really good, you could ask if you can have them framed.

Cards are fun to make for birthdays or Christmas. If you are sending out party invitations, these could have a car theme, too. There could be a drawing with a message underneath. Or you can make a folded card with a picture on the front and a written message inside. Make sure you have envelopes of the right size before you begin.

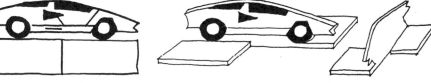

If you would like to make cutouts of cars that will stand up, remember to leave a small piece of cardboard at the bottom as shown. If you bend part of this back and part of it forward, the vehicle will then stand up. You can make a whole range of model cars.

Visit the library and bookshops, and try to find out all you can about the cars of yesterday and today. Then, tomorrow, see how many different types of vehicles you can spot in two minutes while on the way to school (but don't miss that bus!).

©DIAGRAM

Part 3

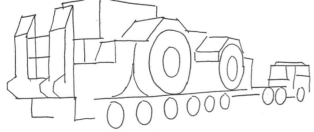

DRAWING VEHICLES IS AN EASY RIDE!

In this part of the book you will find out how to draw everything from a simple family car to a heavy-duty lowloader, like the one shown here, for transporting huge construction machines.

You can see how Peter started to make the drawing with the sketches below. First he looked at the basic shape and thought of it as lots of blocks joined together. Then he thought about which areas had to be dark and which should be light. The vehicle is at an interesting angle and is driving into the distance. That's why the part nearest to us looks so much bigger.

As he drew, Peter kept looking back at the whole shape and was careful about drawing the edges where the various parts dip down and then go up again.

Read on to find out how you, too, can start to think of trucks and cars as circles, oblongs, triangles and squares all joined up together.

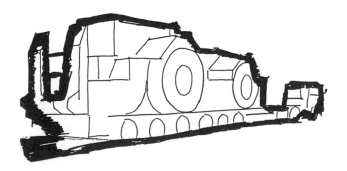

©DIAGRAM

Basic shapes

On these two pages, I have taken lots of circles, squares, oblongs, and curves and joined them up to show you how easy it is to make all sorts of vehicles from these basic shapes.

Take some sticky shapes, if you have some, and try this out for yourself. Or you could cut out lots of different shapes from red, green, yellow or blue paper, plan how to arrange them in the shape of a truck or car, and then stick them down onto another sheet.

Try drawing a sports car using an oblong, two triangles and two circles. Then shade it in, and perhaps add a number to its side.

Tracing shapes

Many of the pictures of vehicles you would like to copy probably have lots of detail in them. A good trick is to forget about this when you start to draw. Instead, think only about the basic outline.

Tracing the outline of any car or truck you are trying to copy will help with this. Before I copied this 1920s delivery truck below, I did the basic outline sketch underneath it. I also did the same thing before I drew the heavy-duty truck designed for desert travel, opposite.

There is also a simple side view of this truck on page 71.

Get some paper and try your hand at tracing or copying the basic outlines of these two vehicles, too. Later, you can have fun putting in all the details like the drivers and texture of the wheels.

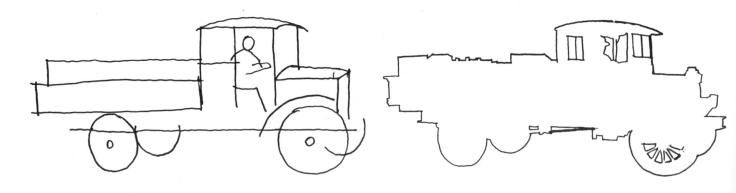

A heavy-duty truck for desert travel.

The outline of a vehicle usually has clues to the overall shape. It can be long and low, short and fat, smooth or jagged. Seeing overall shapes helps you to draw more accurately.

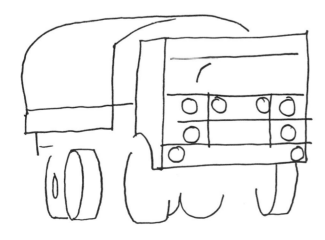

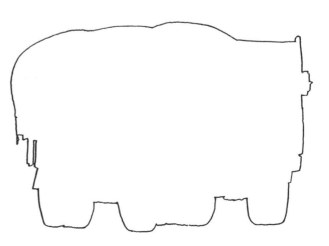

©DIAGRAM

Silhouettes

Now that you have got used to copying or tracing only the outlines of vehicles, you can shade them in to make silhouette pictures that are solid black, without any detail.

If you have copied a side or front view of a car or truck, it will probably be easy to recognize its silhouette when you have shaded it in. But if you have chosen an unusual view – from above perhaps – it might be more difficult to spot what the object is when you have finished.

What sort of vehicles do you think the
silhouettes on these two pages show? Each
shape is of a vehicle somewhere in this
book. Can you find them?

Points of view

To help you think about what a vehicle looks like from the front, back, side and top, here are four drawings of a Russian army jeep. Lots of army jeeps have patterns drawn on them for camouflage. This means that they will not be easily seen because from a distance they look like part of the countryside.

You could try drawing a jeep from all these different points of view, too.

Model-making kits often have plans and elevations (that means side views) of vehicles. Why not try to draw this jeep in the same style as the one on page 74?

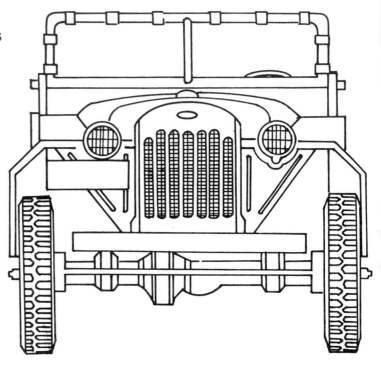

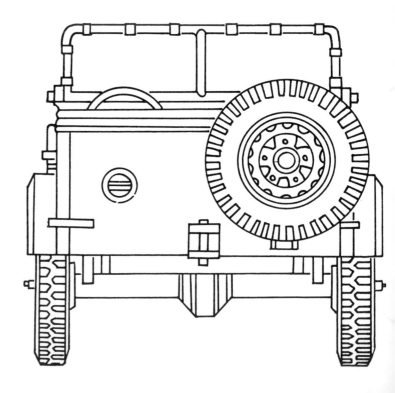

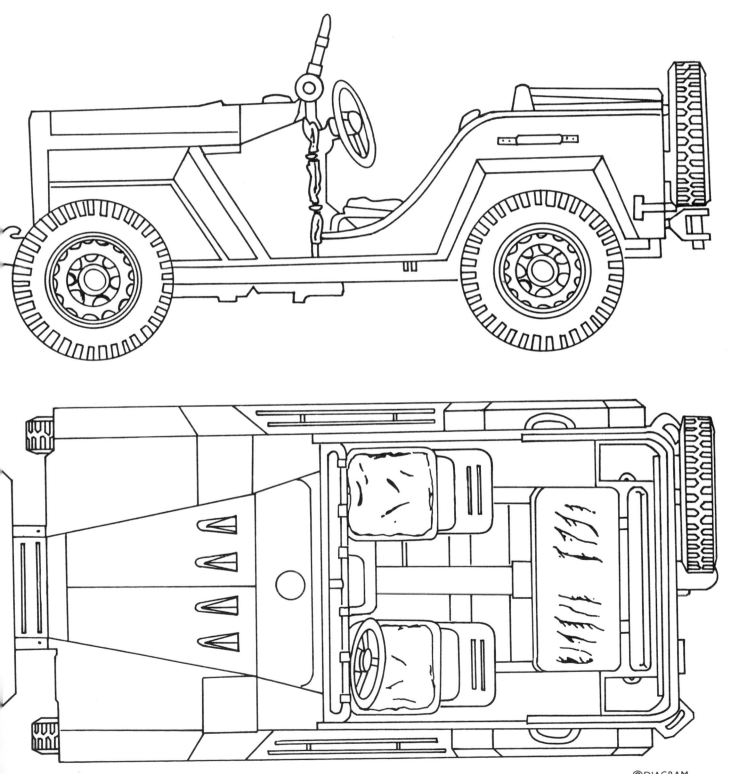

Basic blocks

We have already tried thinking about cars and other vehicles being made up from circles, oblongs, and triangles. But you can make your drawings look more realistic if you now start to think of the various parts as solid blocks like boxes and tubes.

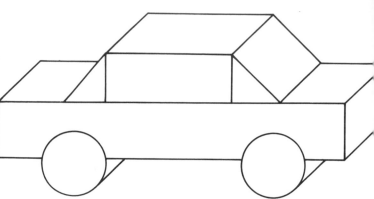

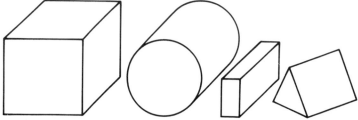

First try drawing a few block shapes like those shown here. Once you have mastered this, you can start to draw whole vehicles in this way.

Take a look at the car on pages 106–107. The final drawing has been built up in a number of stages, but the first ones were simple boxes with the position of the wheels clearly marked, although you only see two of them in the final picture, of course.

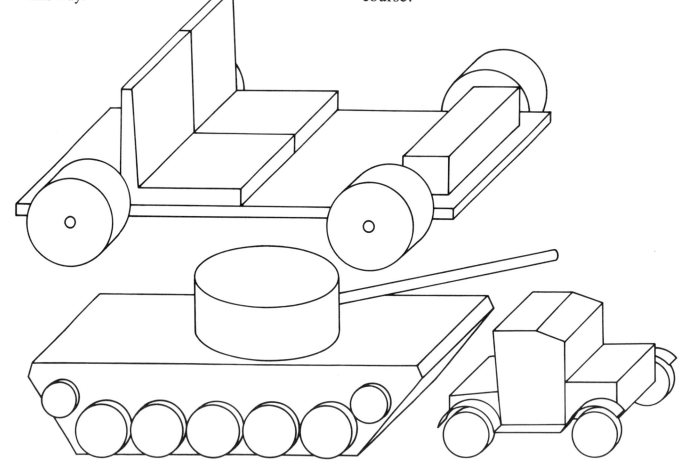

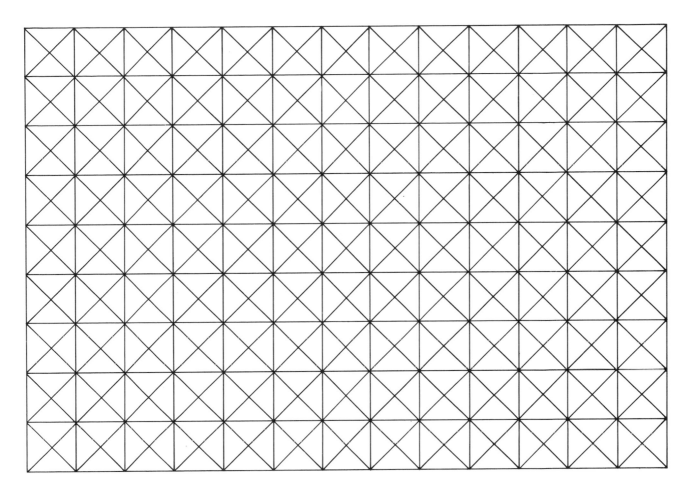

Here is a grid to help you draw basic block vehicles. Place tracing paper over this, and use the diagonal lines to help you with your drawing.

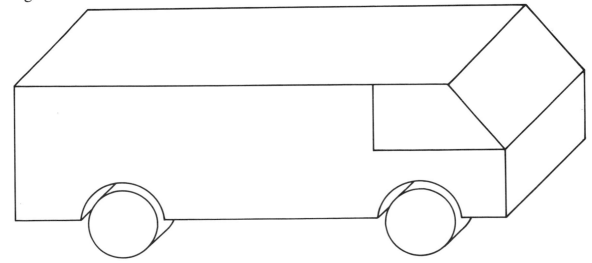

Dazzle and shine

Most cars have shiny parts because the paintwork and the chromium surfaces reflect light. These models have bodies that their owners must have polished until they dazzled.

When you are drawing a car, think carefully about its shiny surfaces. You can easily get a shiny look by using a soft pencil (grade B) and filling in some areas to look very dark but leaving other parts white. Take care not to smudge your drawing when you do this. It helps to put a clean piece of paper under your hand while you are working to protect your picture.

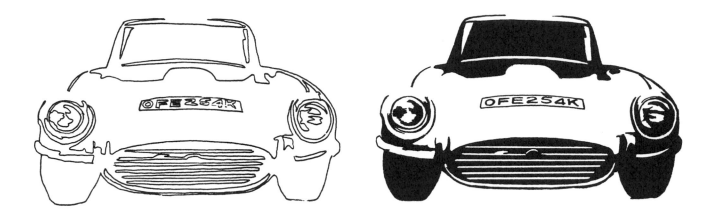

Highly polished

Here are some more cars with a really glossy look for you to copy. Look carefully, remember, to see which areas you should leave white.

This is a four-door Polara. The model below it is a Camaro, dating from 1970.

The Pontiac convertible dates from 1950.

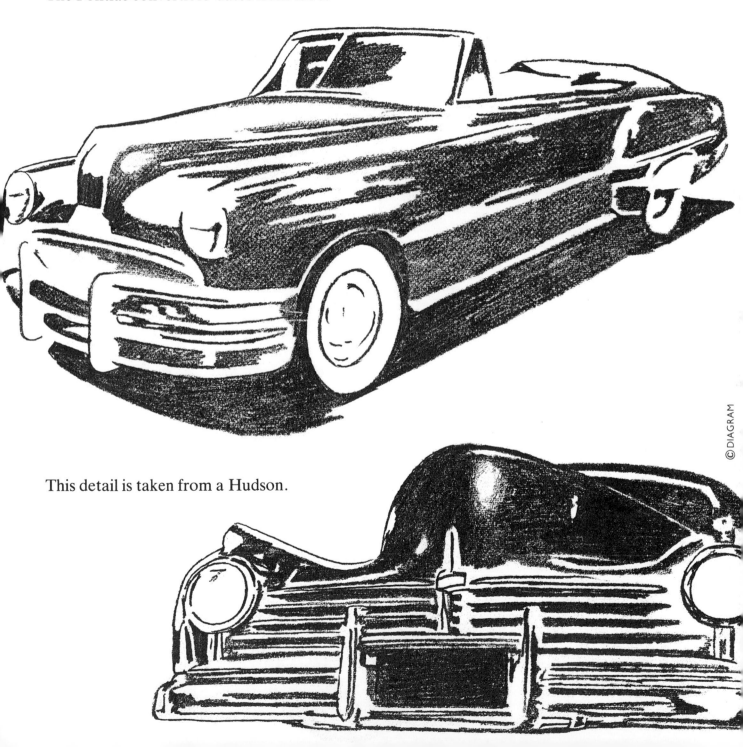

This detail is taken from a Hudson.

©DIAGRAM

High-speed techniques

If you would like to give your pictures the
effect of speed, work with a soft pencil
(grade B), as in the drawings on this page,
and use fast strokes as you sketch. The car
itself does not have to be complete. The
idea is to create the feeling that it is going
by in a flash. Notice how the car at the
bottom of this page seems to be going more
slowly because there is more detail in the
picture.

The car above also looks as if it is moving fast – but this time it is because of the lines drawn under it. The car below, however, looks as if it is parked. There is no sense of movement at all, is there?

Put tracing paper over the Ford below and copy the main shape but make the car look as if it is racing along.

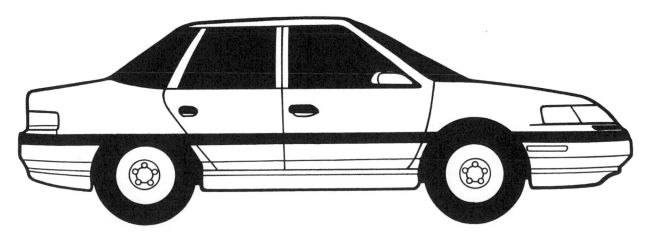

Part 4

Now it's time to start drawing lots of vehicles in easy step-by-step stages. On the pages that follow you will find a whole gallery of various vehicles to copy. You can add your own details — mirrors, spotlights and so on — later.

YOUR VEHICLE GALLERY

Have fun drawing rows and rows of vehicles just as if they were in a traffic jam. Or give your pictures of trucks a construction site in the background; or perhaps draw a car in a sales showroom, or even in a crash!

Step-by-step

You first need to decide whether you want to use a pencil, ink or paints to work with, and choose the best sort of paper. For more information about types of paper, see pages 40–41.

Prop up the book while you are working so that you do not need to keep opening it while you are copying and will not lose the page. If you come to a part that you find difficult, take your time. Draw slowly, and take care over details once you have your basic shape.

Now you can start to draw the German BMW 320i shown opposite, or any other model you wish.

Use a soft pencil (grade B or 2B) to plan your drawing because you will be able to rub out the pencil marks if you make a mistake.

Follow the step-by-step stages shown here. You will notice that I have made some of the lines thicker than others. All **your** lines should be the same thickness. My thicker lines are just to show you what I have added at each step.

You can draw the car any size, but remember that all the parts must be in proportion. That means, for example, that the width of the door of the car shown here always has to be about one-third of the car's length, however large you draw it.

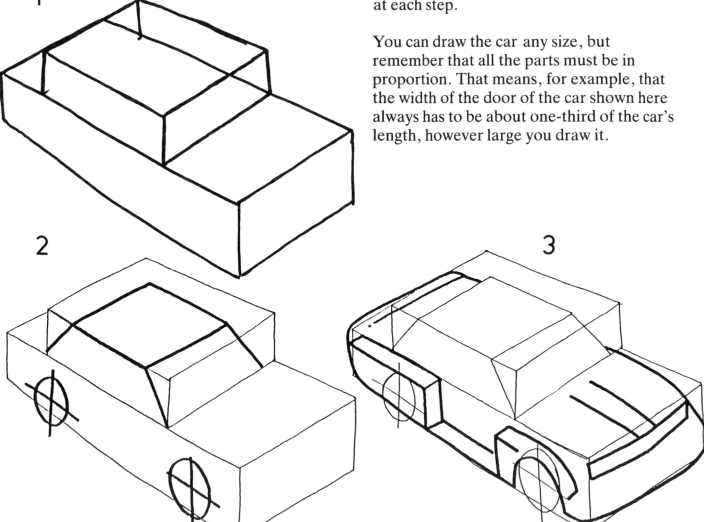

1

2

3

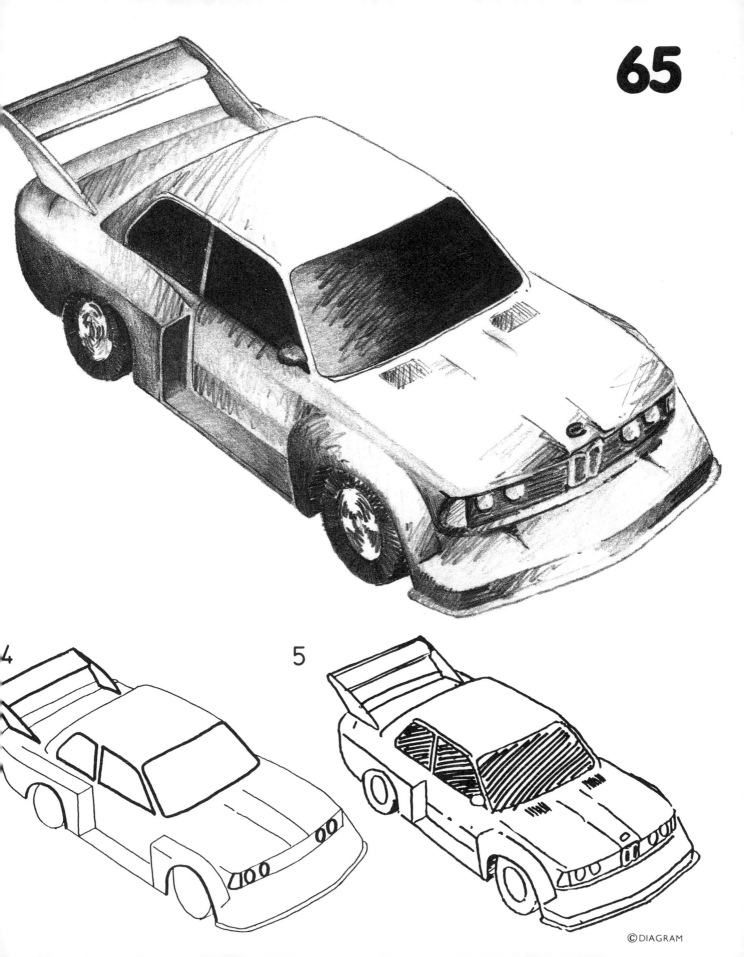

4

5

From the side

Here are some of the different vehicles in this section of the book, all drawn from the side. As you can see, they are not drawn to scale: the motorbike looks as big as the cement mixer, but of course it is not!

Pick up a pencil, and try to draw each of these vehicles, one by one, as simple boxes, triangles and circles or tubes. Even though the last one on the page opposite – a fire engine – may look very complicated, it is still made up from a few basic shapes.

Mirror images

Here are three views of a Ford delivery van for you to copy. In the first picture, it is coming toward us, and the driver is at the wheel. Notice that it is a lefthand drive. (Which side of the road to they drive on in Australia? And Canada? And France?)

In the second picture, the back doors have been opened so that you can see that the vehicle is really just a simple box on wheels.

In the third drawing, the side doors have been opened and you can see the whole length of the vehicle.

When you are drawing cars and trucks, always remember that if you were to cut them down the middle, from the front to the back, each half would be the same – apart from the fact that only one side has a steering wheel. This means that the right headlight must be the same size as the left headlight. In other words, one side matches the other exactly.

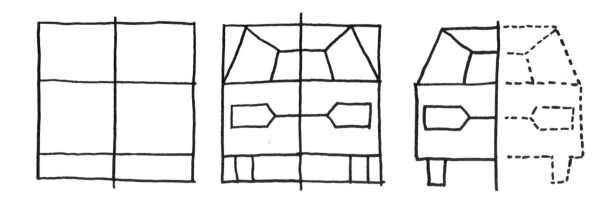

It can be very helpful when you are drawing from different points of view to have small models of cars from which to copy. You can turn them to any angle, and draw them from above or even below if you put them on a glass shelf or turn them upside down.

Below are four simple stages to help you draw a side view of the van.

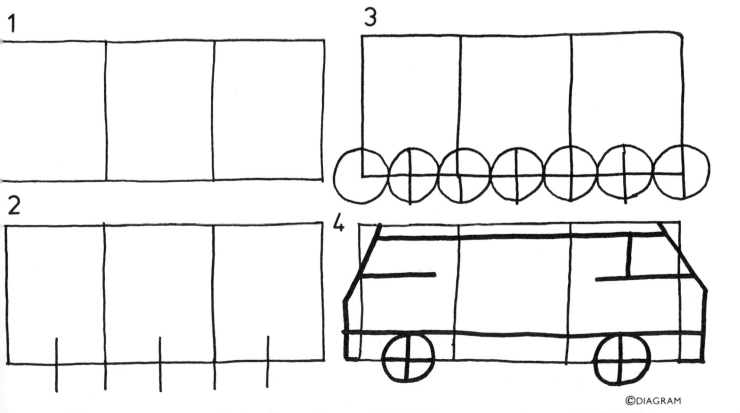

1

2

3

4

Boxes on wheels

This is a 1920s delivery truck, and it's very easy to draw, if you follow the simple stages opposite. As you can see its basic construction is based on eight squares, each of which is the width of one wheel.

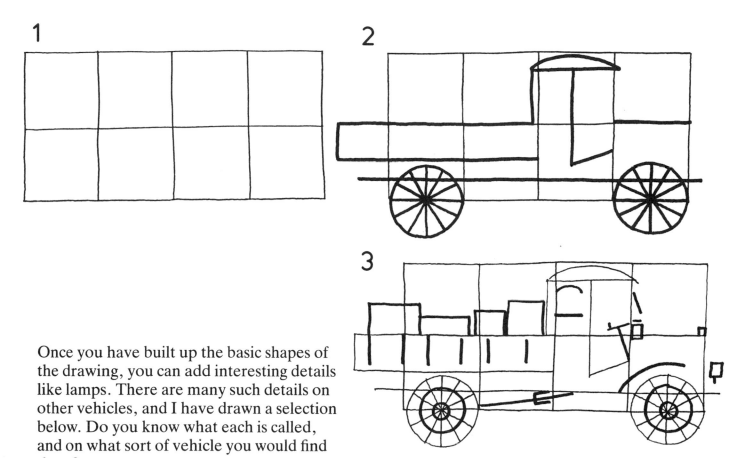

1

2

3

Once you have built up the basic shapes of the drawing, you can add interesting details like lamps. There are many such details on other vehicles, and I have drawn a selection below. Do you know what each is called, and on what sort of vehicle you would find them?

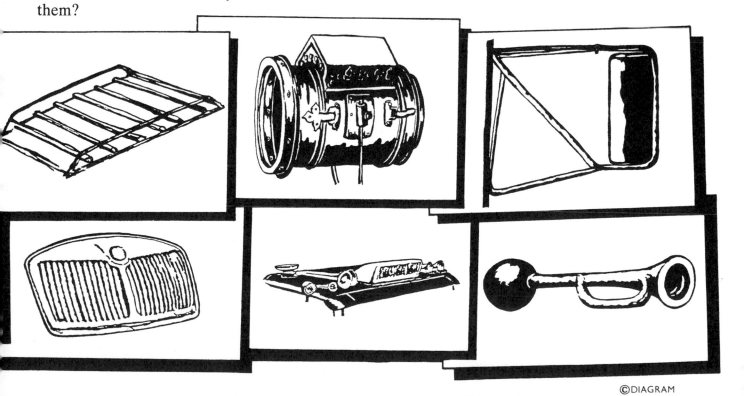

Vintage models

1

2

3

4

It is really quite easy to draw this 1920s cabriolet (say *cab-ree-oh-lay*), which has its door about to be opened by a chauffeur.

The various stages are shown below. Wait until you have the basic shape before you position the chauffeur.

Notice that the part of the car where the chauffeur would sit was not covered. This meant that he always had to wear warm clothes.

It can be very interesting to look through newspapers and magazines for pictures of old or vintage cars like this one. Many look very different from the cars of today.

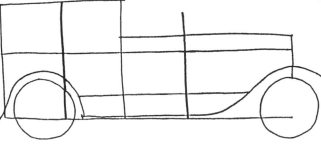

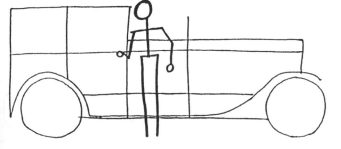

Reminder!
Don't forget to check that the spare wheel is drawn the same size as the other two that you can see. You could also add a face in the window of someone about to get out.

Army vehicles

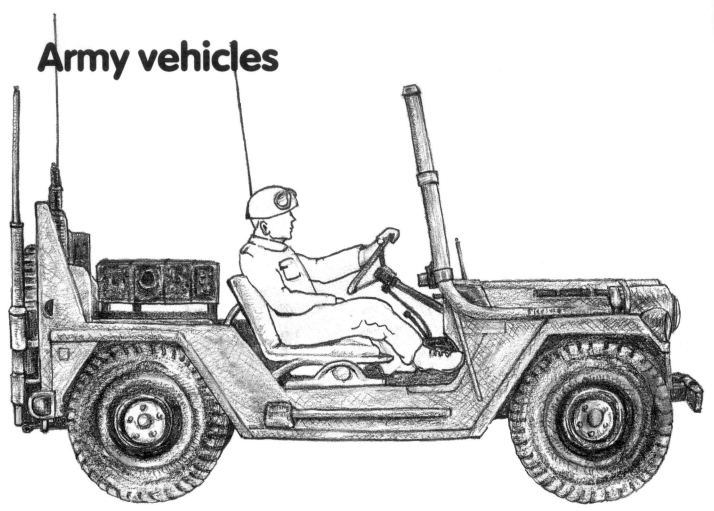

This is the sort of jeep once widely used by the United States Marine Corps.

As you start to copy the step-by-step stages shown opposite, check carefully that the distance between the wheels is right or the vehicle will look strange. The length of the jeep is about four wheels in all. But the distance between the front and back wheels is less than two wheel spaces, as shown below.

But not all vehicles have the same space between the wheels. Did you notice that the delivery van, on page 69, had a two-and-a-half wheel space between the front and back wheels?

Notice how rough the wheels are on the jeep, just as they should be in a vehicle that has to cross rugged land.

There are top, front and back views of a similar jeep on pages 52–53.

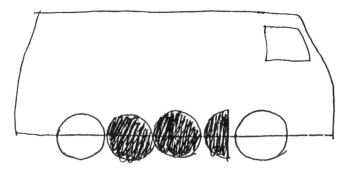

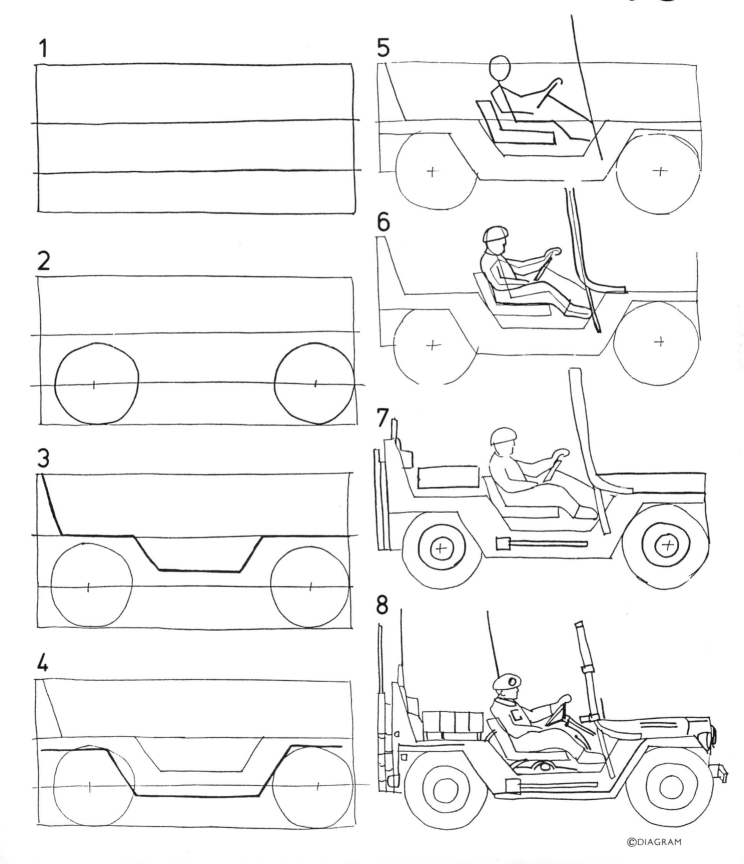

75

Model T Ford

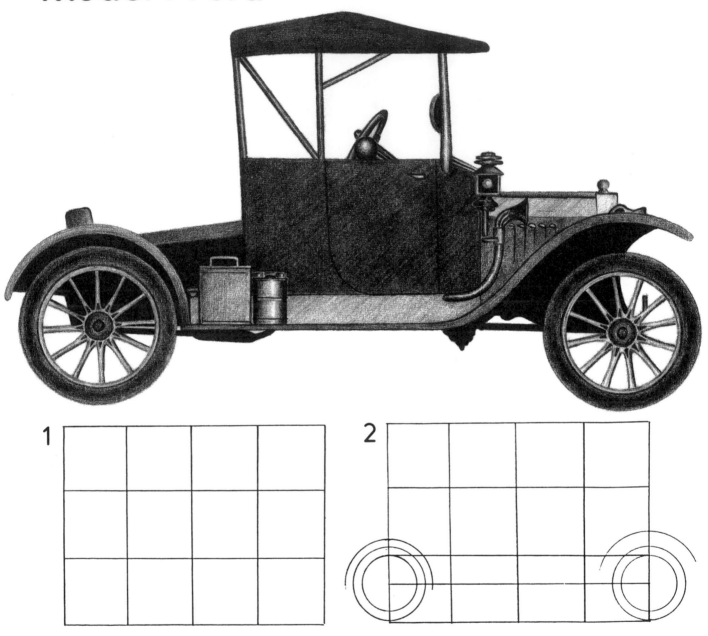

1

2

This is a side view of a Model T Ford, which you can follow in step-by-step stages. It was first introduced in 1908, but this model dates from 1923. You will probably never see one on the road today, but you might spot one at a vintage car rally or in a car museum.

You will find another view of it on page 130.

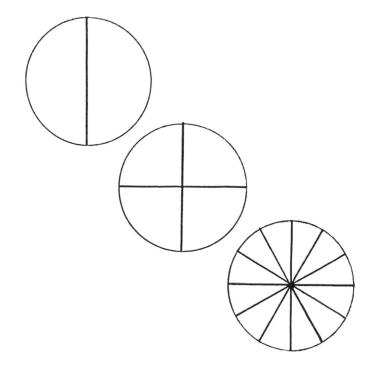

To draw the correct positions of the spokes you have to divide the wheel into twelve equal wedge-shaped parts. First draw a straight line from top to bottom, through the middle of a circle. Then a line from side to side through the middle, so the two lines form an even cross of four parts. Now guess (yes, use your judgment) to divide each quarter into three equal parts.

You can use a ruler, but work with a soft pencil and try the divisions on a piece of paper before working on your finished drawing.

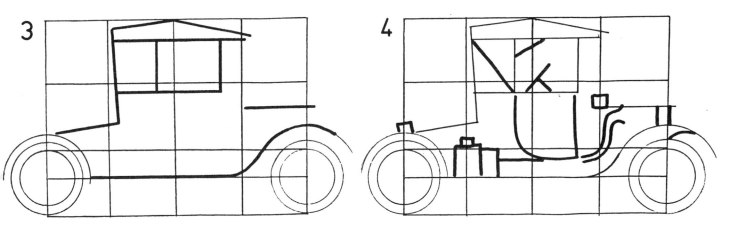

- Use a pair of compasses to help you draw the circles.
- Put a piece of cardboard under your drawing when using compasses so that they do not slip.
- Remember when you are copying to keep checking the size of details like wheels and doors. Keep checking that you are putting everything in its right place.
- Always use a soft pencil for your first lines. You can easily rub out these if you make a mistake.
- Keep the ruler you use for drawing straight lines clean or it may smudge your drawings. If you use it when drawing with felt-tips, wipe the edge afterwards.

A family hatchback

This is a small two-door family car, with trim, tidy lines, which is easy to draw. Again, you can build it up from a series of simple boxes, as shown here. Before you position the wheels, try guessing how many wheel spaces there are between the front and back ones by looking at the final drawing.

This is the family car of today. But what do you think cars will be like in fifty years' time? Turn to pages 136–137 where Mary has drawn what she thinks that cars of the future might look like.

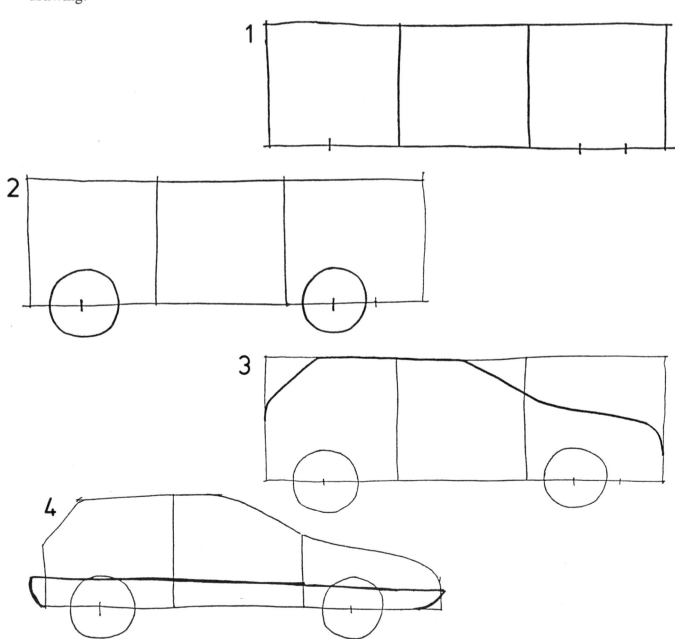

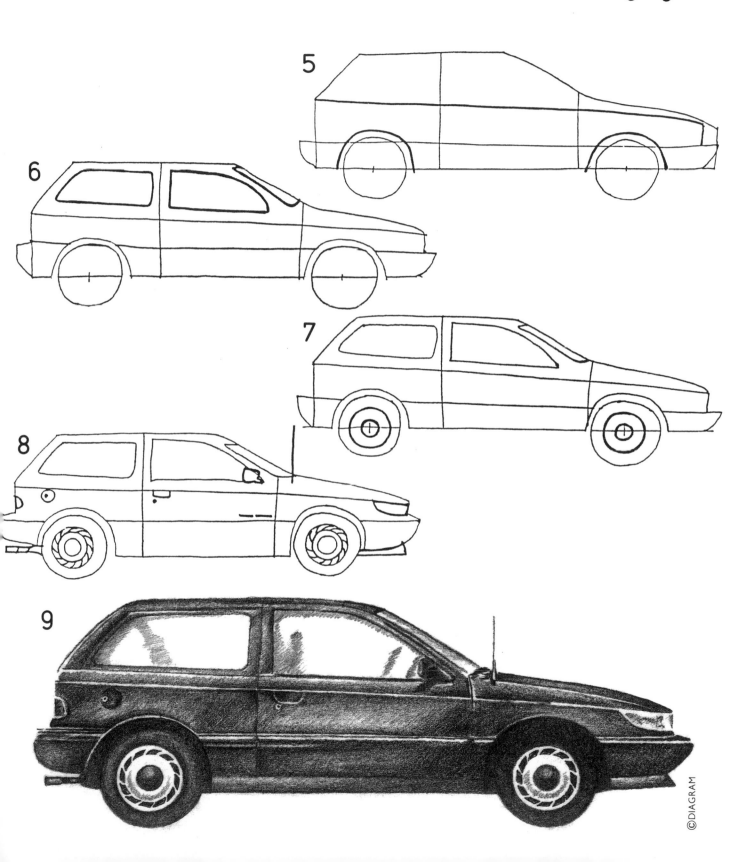

5

6

7

8

9

©DIAGRAM

A sports model

This 1988 Lamborghini (say *Lam-bor-gee-nee*) is a two-seater sports car, built for speed.

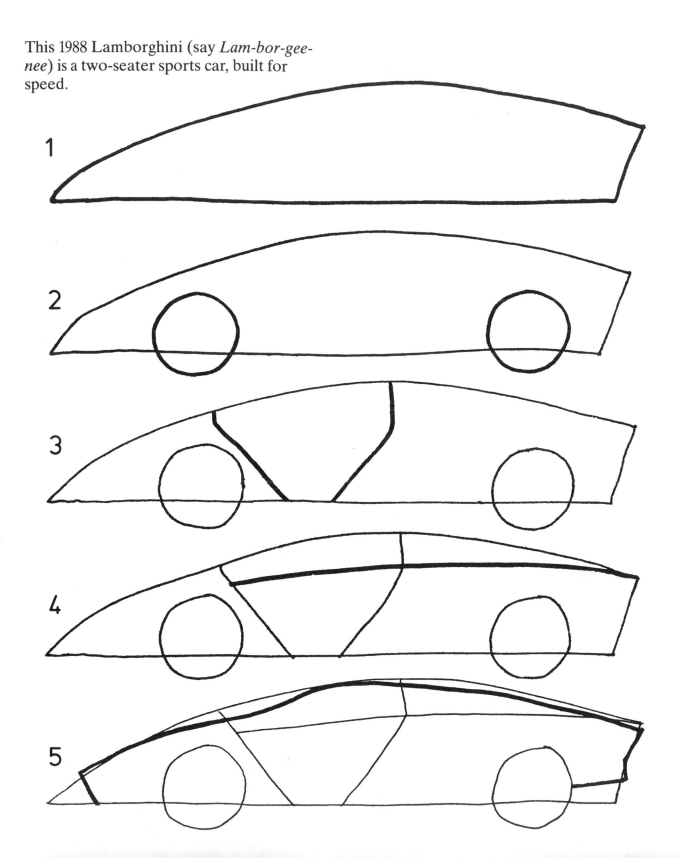

6

7

Graham drew it in step-by-step stages in pencil, and then used a brush for his final drawing. Then, in an extra drawing, to give the effect of speed, he just hinted at the basic shape with a series of lines. You can try a similar technique if you would like to make a drawing of any type of car look as if it is moving. Simply trace any of the vehicles in this book using a very soft pencil to get the basic shape. Then draw in a series of lines, just like Graham has done here. You will have seen, on page 60, how to add speed to your cars.

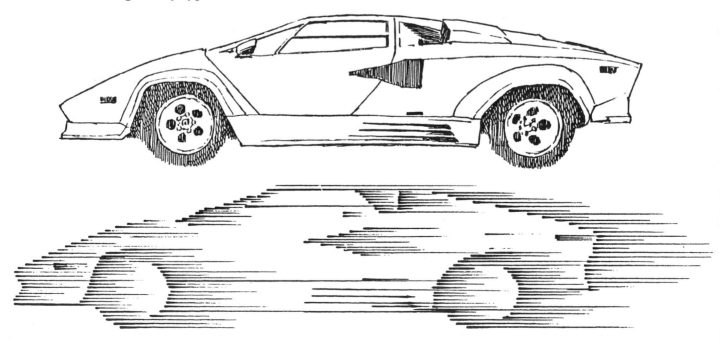

A bird's-eye view

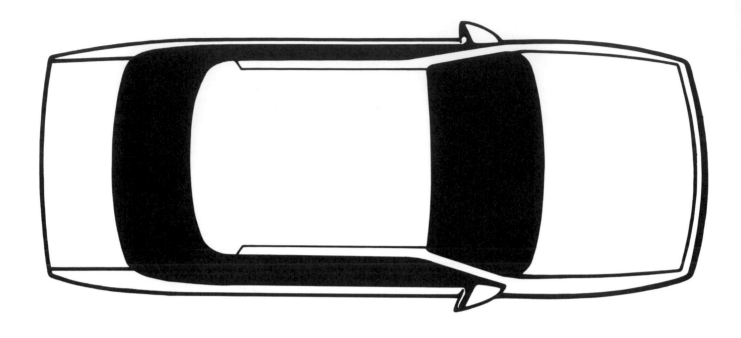

This is a Ford Mercury Sable, shown from above, just as a bird might see it or you might view it from an airplane. Also shown is a straightforward side view.

1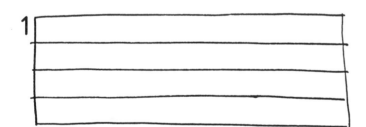

2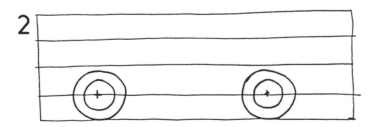

3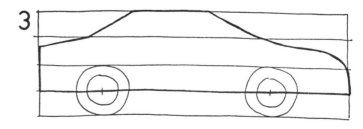

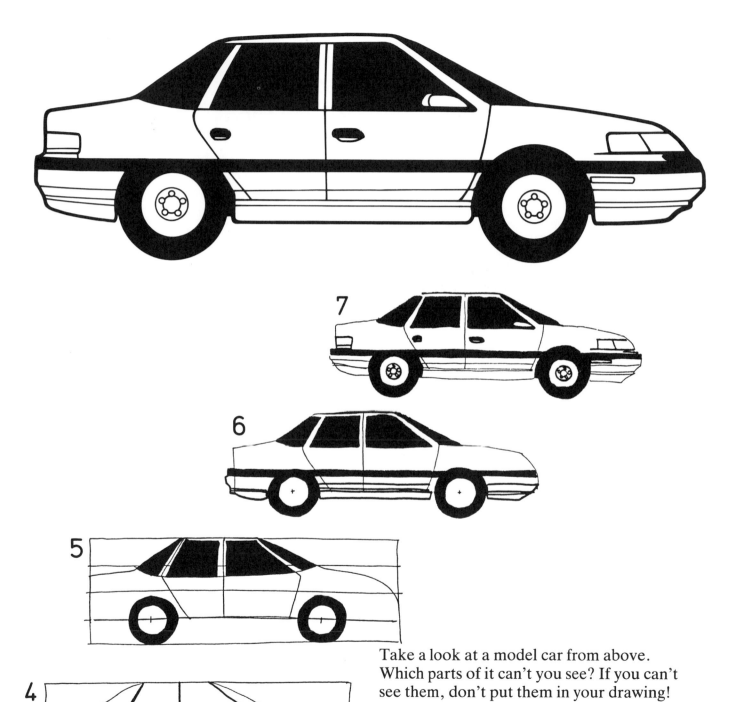

7

6

5

4

Take a look at a model car from above. Which parts of it can't you see? If you can't see them, don't put them in your drawing!

Although modern cars look simple because of their streamlined shapes, they are often harder to draw than an older car which has lots of box-like parts.

Volkswagen Beetle

This car, from Germany, is made up from lots of curves and a few straight lines. It is called a Beetle because of the way it looks. Its name, Volkswagen (the Germans say *folks-varg-en*), means "people's car".

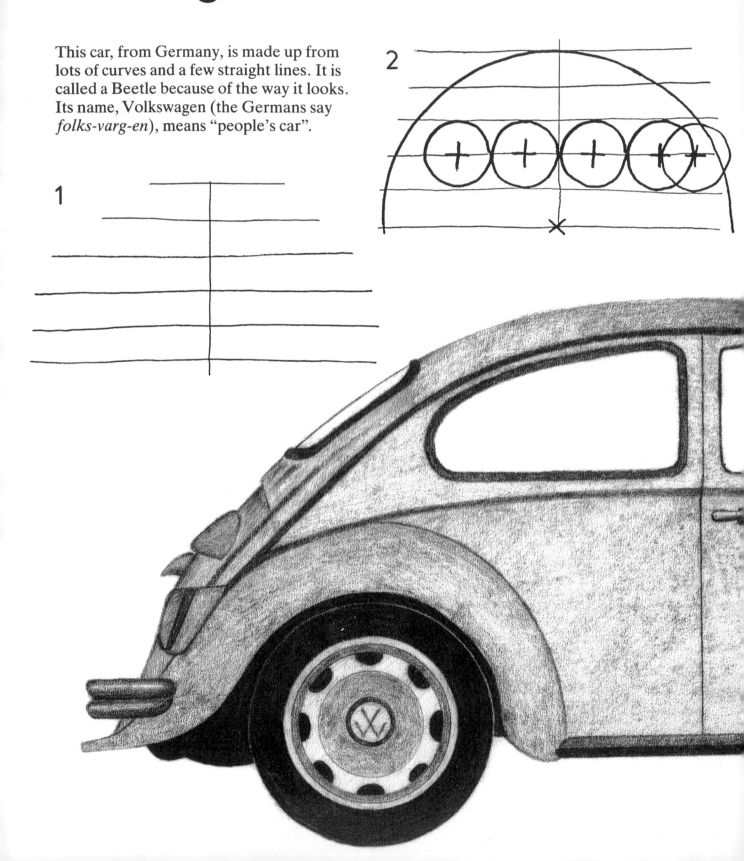

Follow these step-by-step stages carefully. To help you get the right amount of space between the front and the back wheels, I have put in three extra imaginary wheels of the same size. When you have finished your drawing, you can rub these out.

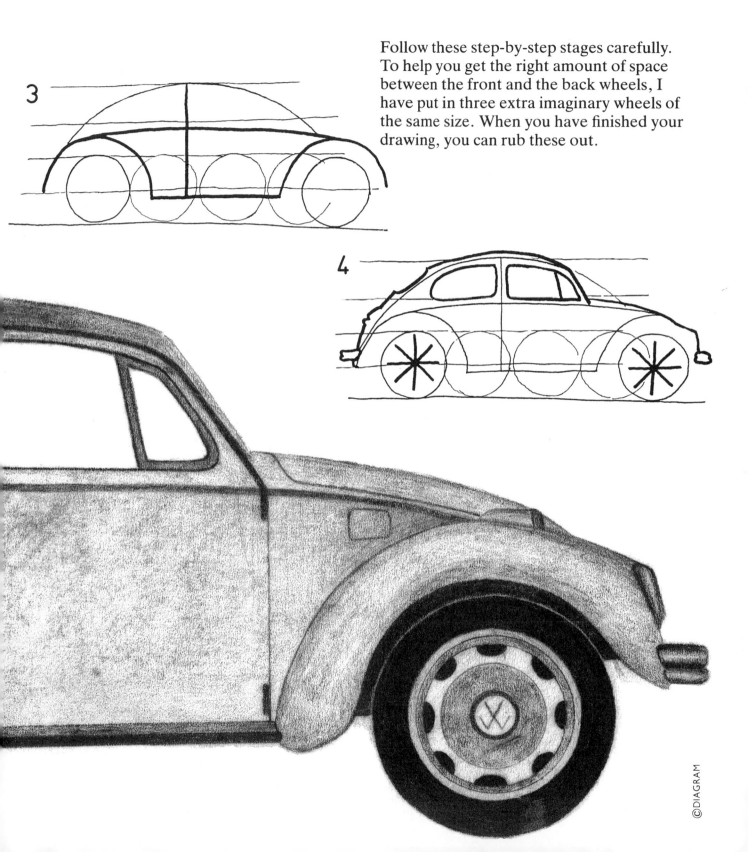

©DIAGRAM

High-speed racer

This superb racing car is made up from lots of straight lines and circles, so a ruler and a pair of compasses will be very useful.

Begin with two rows of nine squares. Then draw the wheels two squares in from either end. Notice that the two wheels are not the same size.

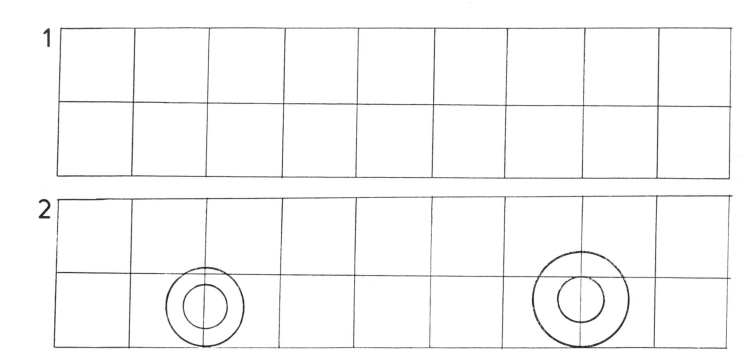

When you have finished your drawing, you can put in lots of lines around it to make this model seem to be going just as fast – or even faster – than the racing car on pages 18–19. Read pages 60–61 to learn this trick.

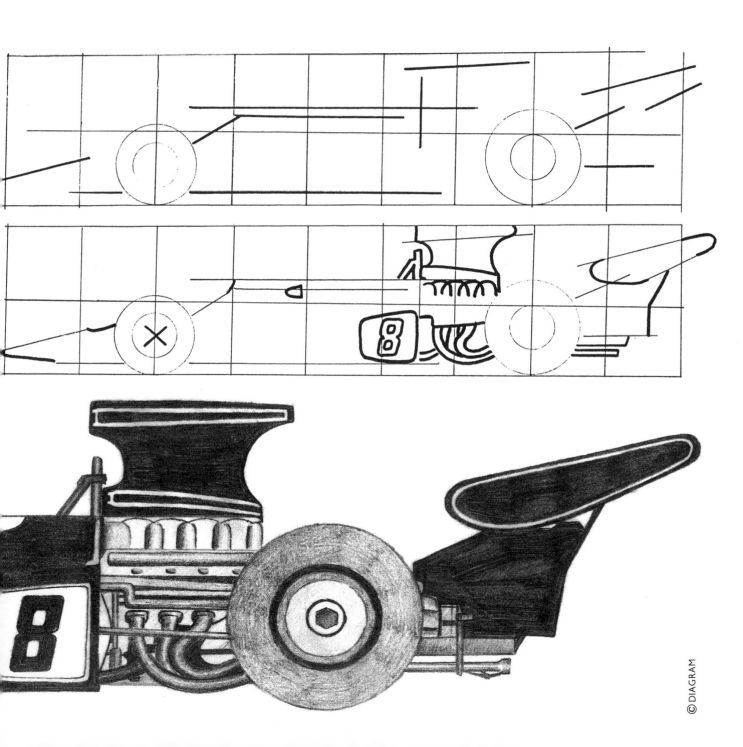

Cement mixer

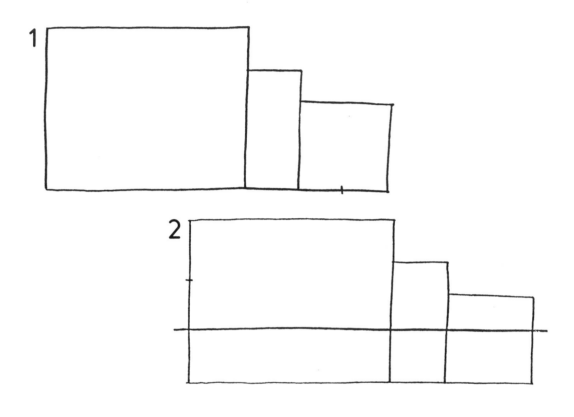

This vehicle is just like the very large one shown on pages 8–9. Here you can see how to draw it in several stages.

First try to think of the vehicle as three oblongs of different sizes, joined together. Then draw a line across to mark the level of the tops of the wheels. Next, mark the position of the three wheels that can be seen with simple circles.

Now mark in the barrel-like shape that contains the cement. Gradually add other details as shown.

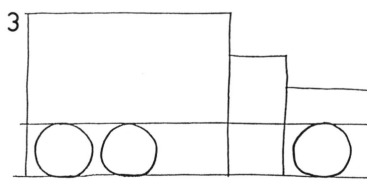

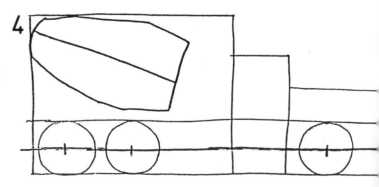

5

Notice that the wheels are heavy-duty. This is because the vehicle probably has to travel through a lot of mud and rough ground on construction sites.

6

7

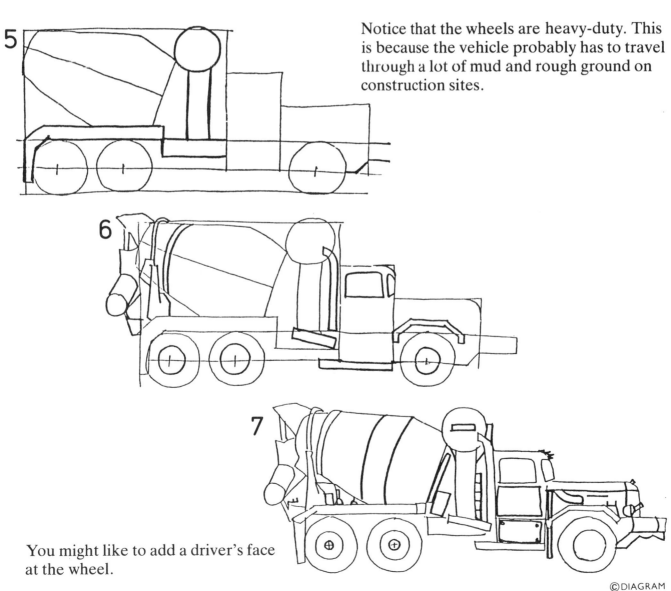

You might like to add a driver's face at the wheel.

©DIAGRAM

Motorbike

The motorbike opposite looks very difficult to draw because of all its many parts. But if, again, you can start to think of it as a number of basic shapes like circles and oblongs, it will be far easier.

This is a Honda CB750. James did the drawing in ten step-by-step stages, copying it from a photograph in a catalogue.

You can collect lots of catalogues from car and bike showrooms to help with your drawings, and also cut out pictures from newspapers and magazines.

You might like to draw a whole range of different sorts of bike if you can find enough pictures to copy.

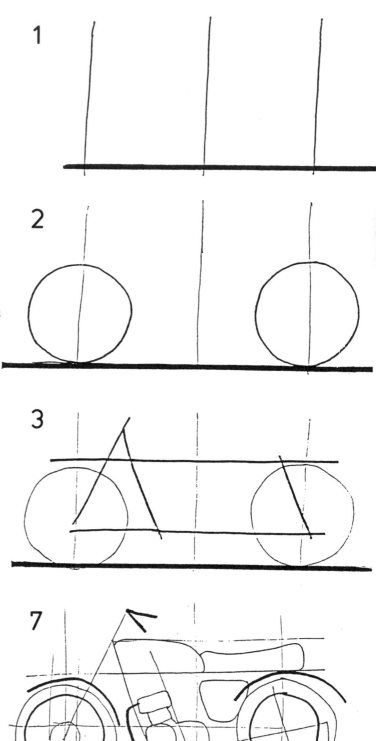

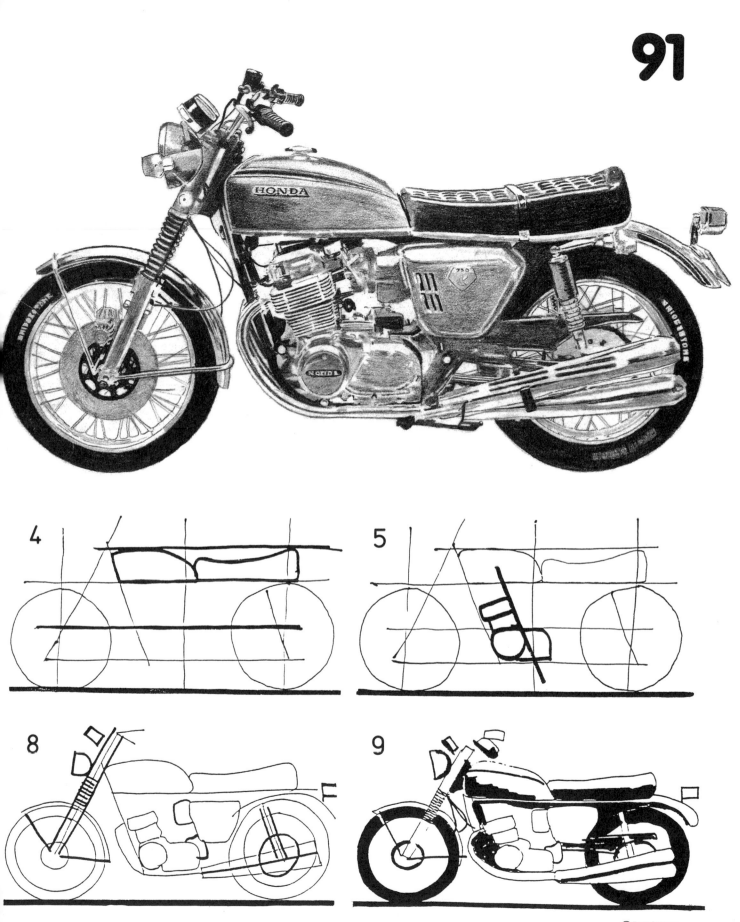

A fire engine

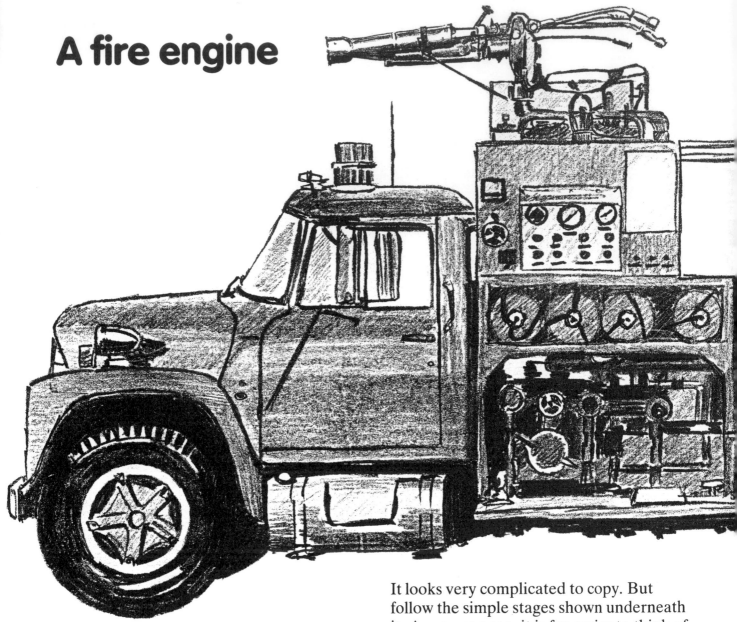

This fire engine, based at an oil refinery, shoots powerful jets of foam from the guns mounted behind the driver's cabin.

It looks very complicated to copy. But follow the simple stages shown underneath it. As you can see, it is far easier to think of the vehicle as lots of different basic shapes that are joined together. Note that there are four wheel spaces between the front and back wheels.

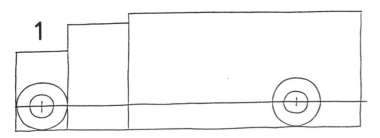

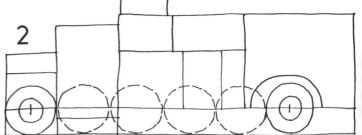

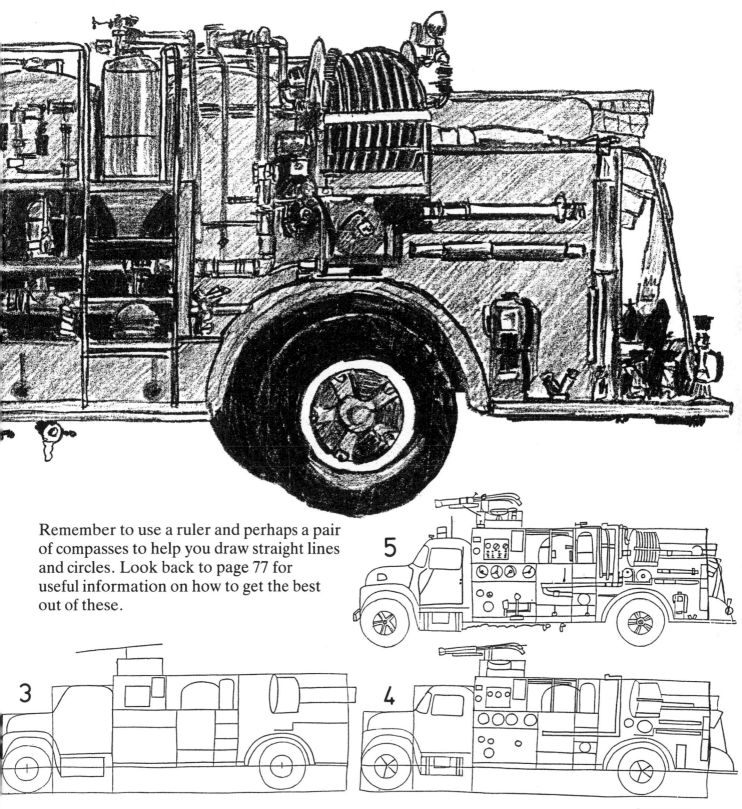

Remember to use a ruler and perhaps a pair of compasses to help you draw straight lines and circles. Look back to page 77 for useful information on how to get the best out of these.

5

3

4

Car-crusher

Car-crushers are monster vehicles built especially to amuse the crowds at fairs and festivals. They have pick-up truck bodies and very powerful engines, as well as huge wheels.

They are not built to race, but with the power of about one thousand horses perform stunts by bashing old cars and other vehicles so that these end up a mass of tangled metal.

1

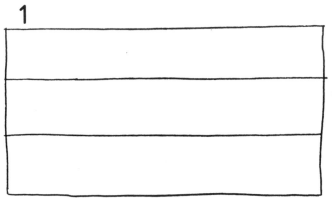

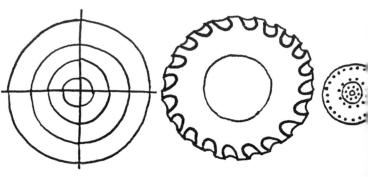

When you draw your wheels, plan them like a target, with smaller circles inside the larger ones. But remember that these crushers have big wheels and the hubs are deep inside.

2

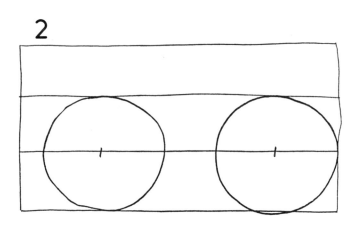

3

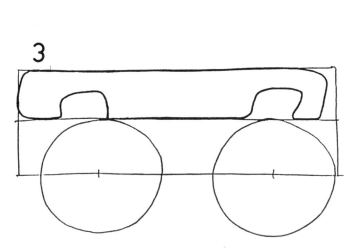

4

Copy the car-crusher shown here. Then put it into a really dramatic picture, crushing any car you like, or don't like.

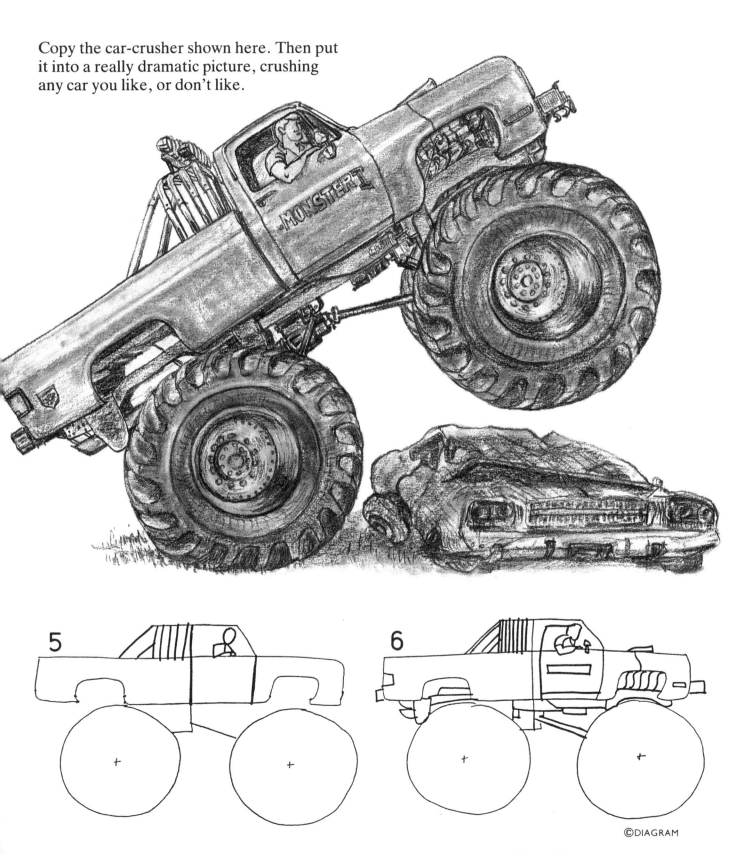

©DIAGRAM

Cord coupé (say *coo-pay*)

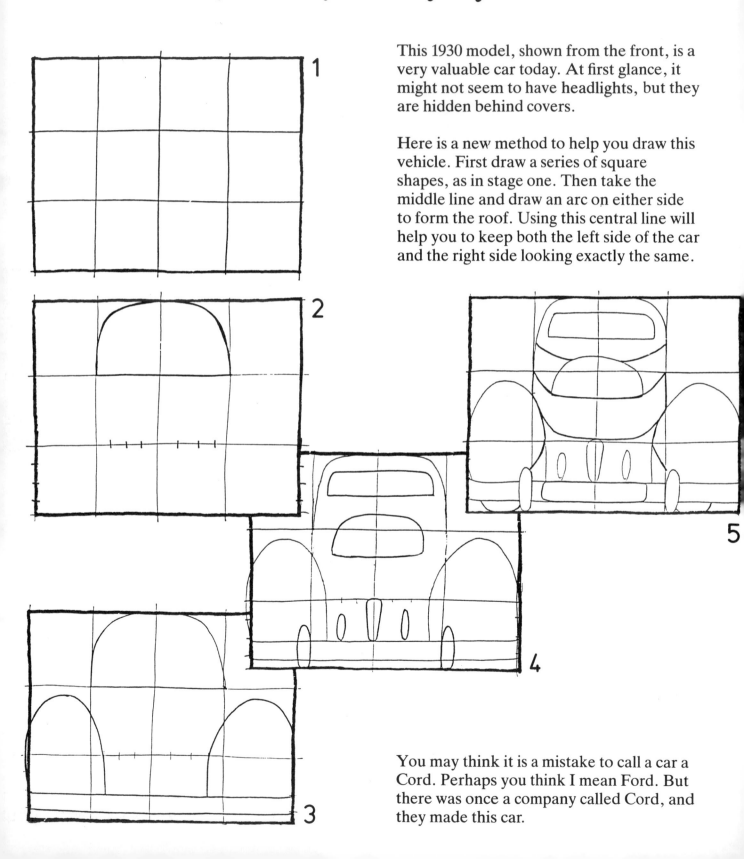

This 1930 model, shown from the front, is a very valuable car today. At first glance, it might not seem to have headlights, but they are hidden behind covers.

Here is a new method to help you draw this vehicle. First draw a series of square shapes, as in stage one. Then take the middle line and draw an arc on either side to form the roof. Using this central line will help you to keep both the left side of the car and the right side looking exactly the same.

You may think it is a mistake to call a car a Cord. Perhaps you think I mean Ford. But there was once a company called Cord, and they made this car.

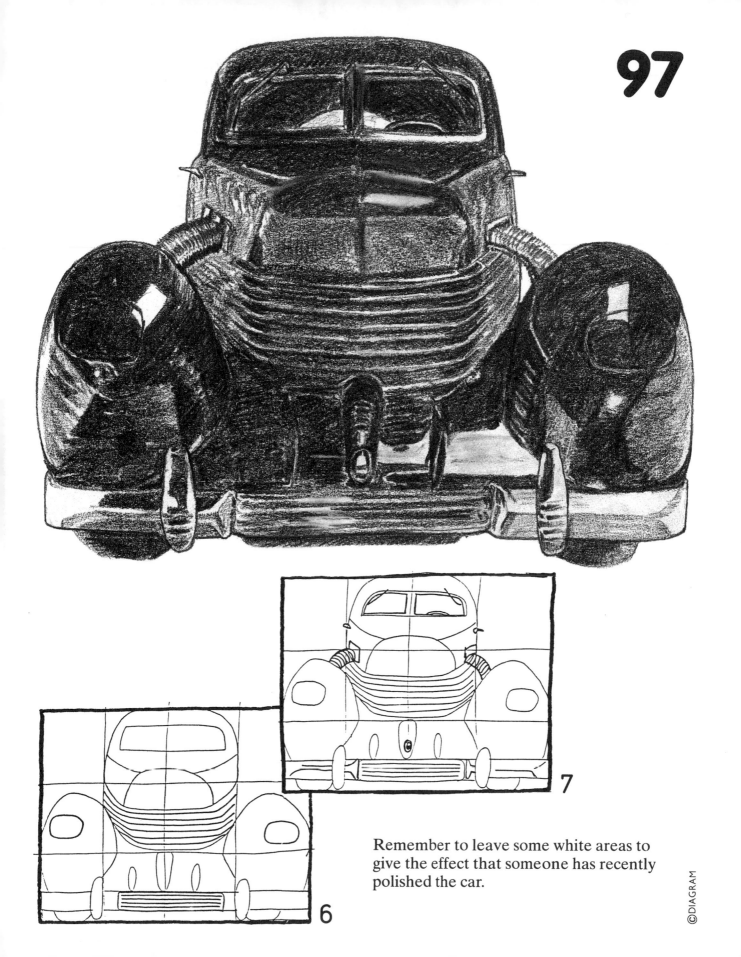

7

6

Remember to leave some white areas to give the effect that someone has recently polished the car.

©DIAGRAM

An army tank

This United States Army tank looks a little
like a ship, and is very simple to draw.
Follow the ten step-by-step stages shown,
making sure that you put in lots of circles
for the many wheels and mark in the chain
that links them.

1

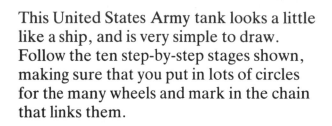

2

3

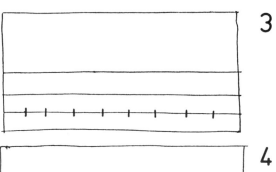

4

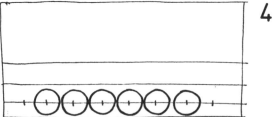

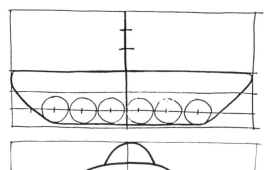

5

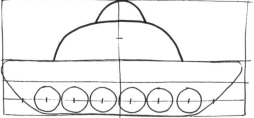

6

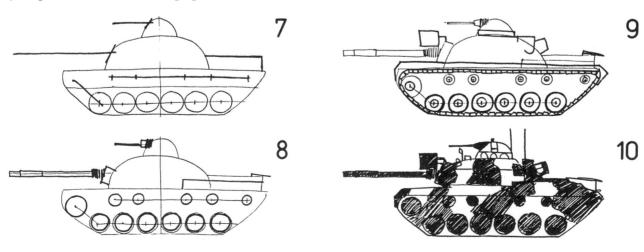

You might also like to put in lots of camouflage markings. These are used so that the tank will not be easily seen by the enemy.

Tips for drawing
● If you would like to draw some rough terrain over which this tank might be moving, place your drawing over a rough surface (sandpaper, a plank of wood or some fabric) and then rub a pencil or crayon over the area you want to be the rocky ground. This will give you a texture like the sandpaper, wood or fabric that you put underneath the paper.

7

8

9

10

Various viewpoints

So far you will have been drawing some vehicles from the front and some from the side. Now it's time to start drawing cars and trucks from some unusual angles.

These two pages show trucks, a family car, a tank, racing cars and a crowd-control van seen either partly from above, or from angles that let you see some of the side and some of the front.

It will help to get you used to drawing from these angles if you trace the outlines of these seven vehicles. Then you can try copying them freehand, once again by dividing each vehicle into different basic shapes like circles and oblongs.

©DIAGRAM

One truck – two viewpoints

On these two pages you can see how to draw the same truck from two different viewpoints in step-by-step stages.

One view shows the side and part of the back. The other shows the front and the side.

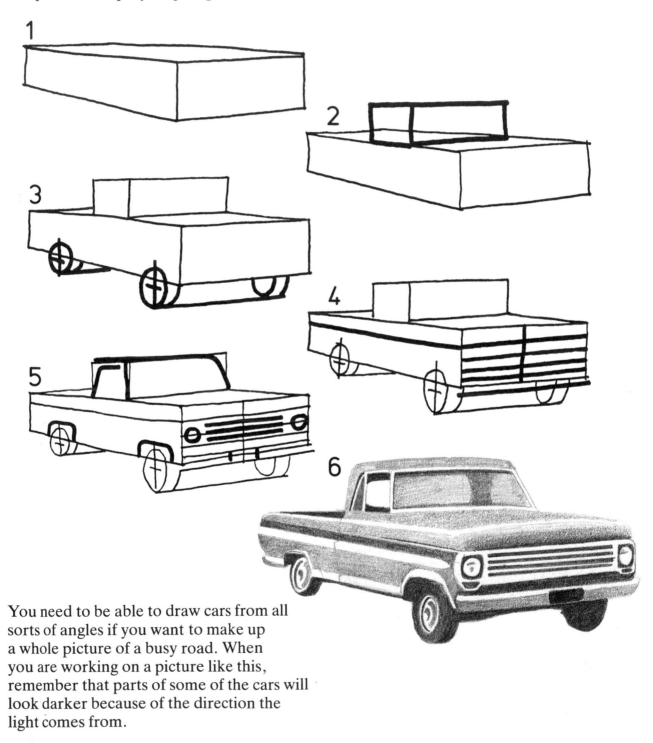

You need to be able to draw cars from all sorts of angles if you want to make up a whole picture of a busy road. When you are working on a picture like this, remember that parts of some of the cars will look darker because of the direction the light comes from.

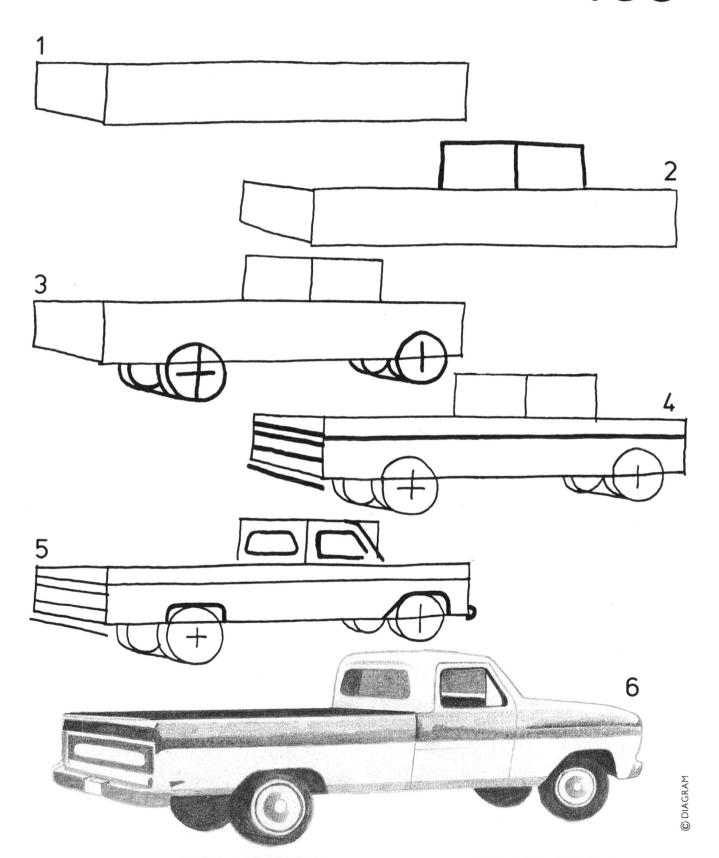

Toyota pick-up truck

Build up the outline from a simple box shape with a tent-like structure on top of it. The truck shown here is a right-hand drive, since it was made for the United Kingdom, but you can change the position of the wheel and the driver if you would like to.

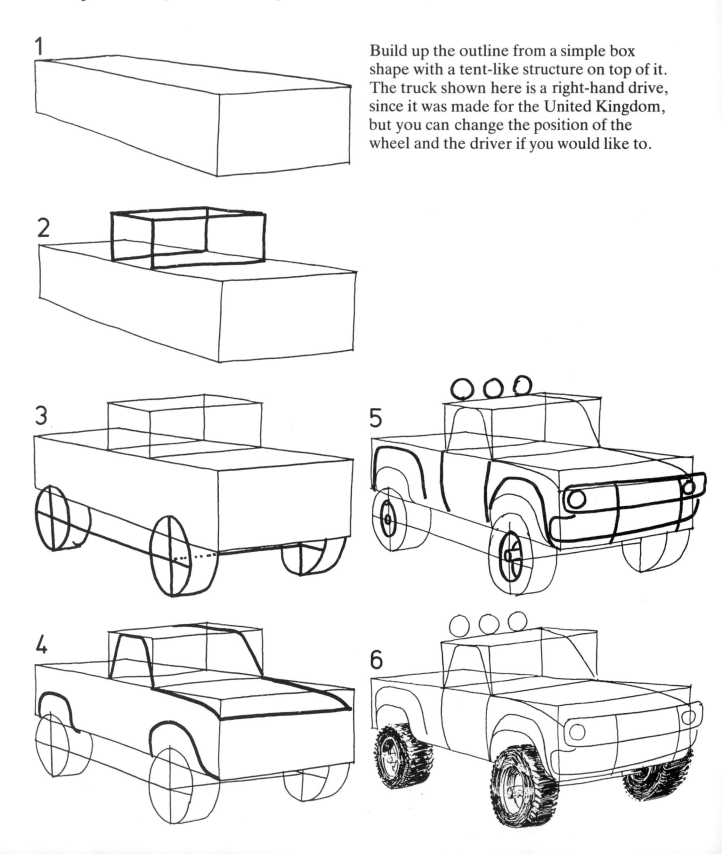

This type of pick-up truck has very chunky wheels. Notice that here they are not drawn from the side but at an angle. This means they do not look exactly like circles but a bit like ovals on their ends, as you can see on page 131.

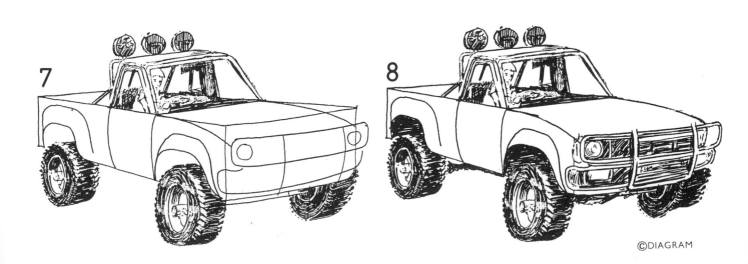

7

8

©DIAGRAM

Leopard TRX

This family car with a sunroof is easily built up into a drawing from two box shapes, the smaller one on top of the larger one. The viewpoint is such that you can see the roof, front and one side. This model has just two doors, and from this angle only one door is seen.

The drawing here was copied from a picture in a toy catalogue which has lots of photographs of model cars. The driver was then added to make the whole thing realistic. You could, of course, add some passengers, too.

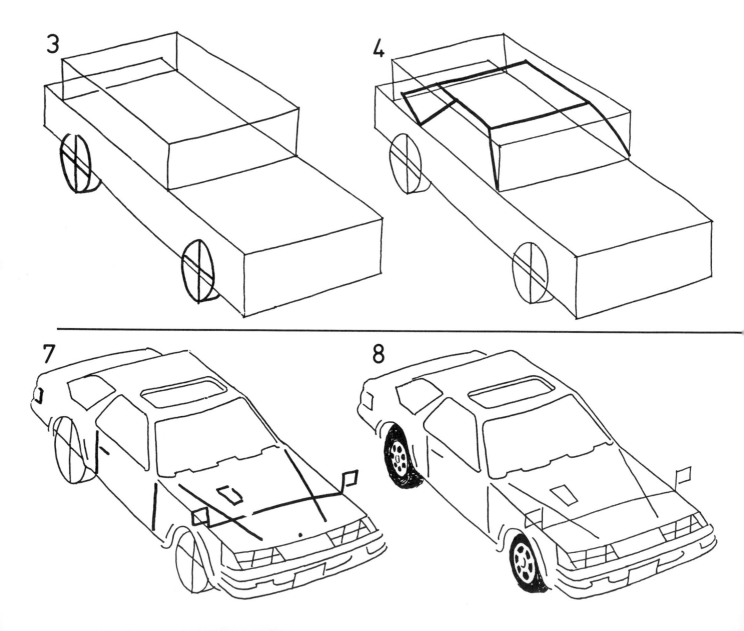

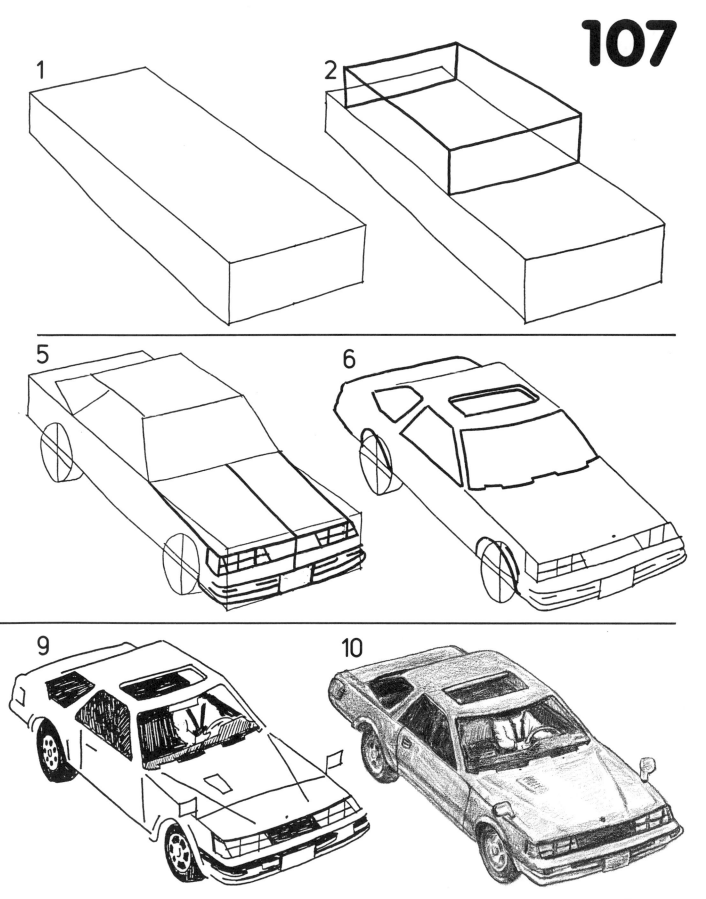

107

1

2

5

6

9

10

©DIAGRAM

A crowd-control van

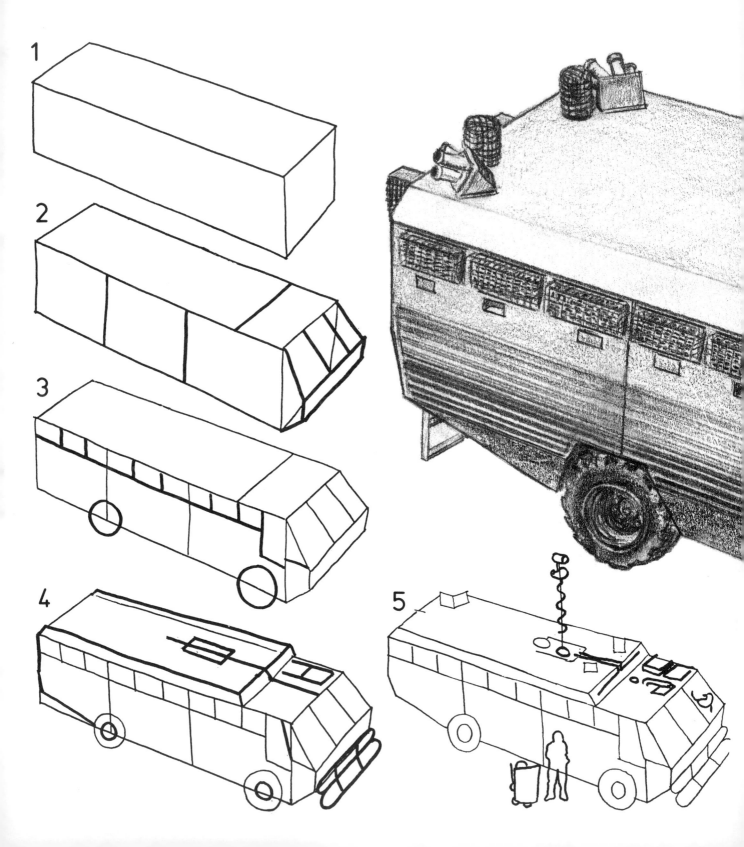

1

2

3

4

5

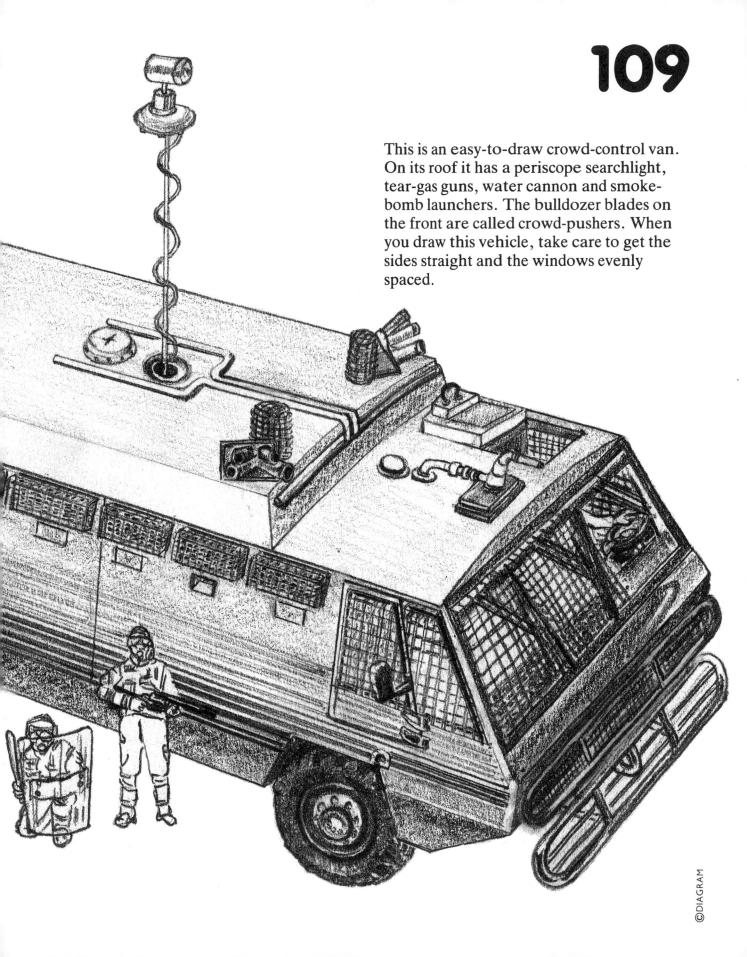

This is an easy-to-draw crowd-control van. On its roof it has a periscope searchlight, tear-gas guns, water cannon and smoke-bomb launchers. The bulldozer blades on the front are called crowd-pushers. When you draw this vehicle, take care to get the sides straight and the windows evenly spaced.

©DIAGRAM

Tank attack!

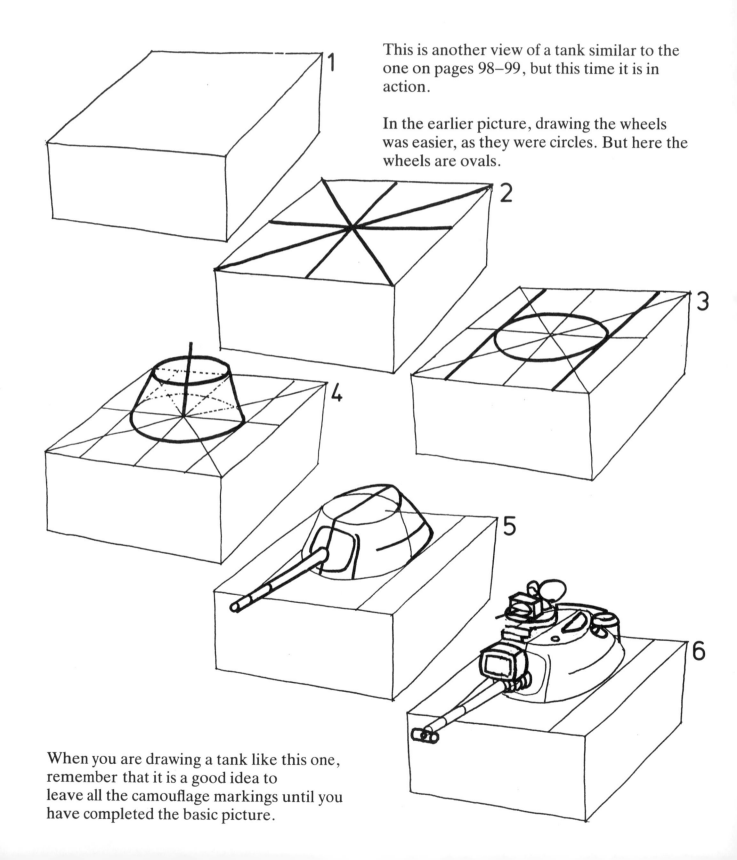

This is another view of a tank similar to the one on pages 98–99, but this time it is in action.

In the earlier picture, drawing the wheels was easier, as they were circles. But here the wheels are ovals.

When you are drawing a tank like this one, remember that it is a good idea to leave all the camouflage markings until you have completed the basic picture.

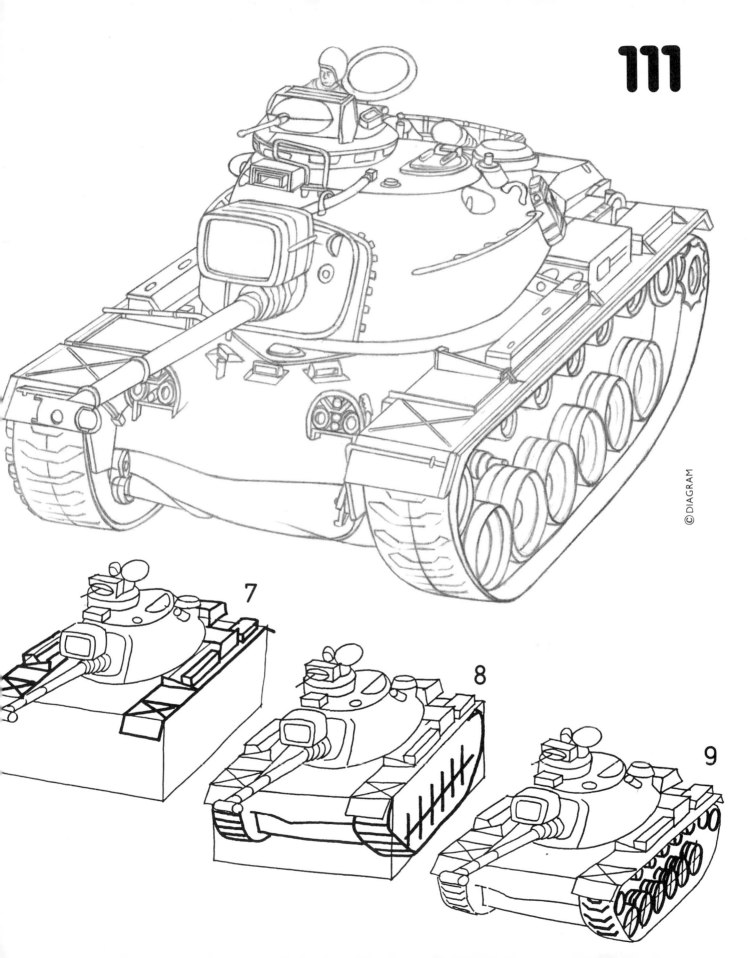

7

8

9

©DIAGRAM

High-speed racing car

This championship racing car is capable of very high speeds. It was drawn by Graham with a brush and black ink after he had sketched a basic outline on thick white paper. Only when he was sure he had everything in the right place did he ink in his drawing. Then, when the ink was dry, he rubbed out the pencil marks so that no one would ever know they had been there.

The viewpoint is as if you are watching a race from way above the track. The areas of solid black give a very good impression of a powerful vehicle with an average speed of over 241 kph (150 mph). (What is the speed limit in the area where you live?)

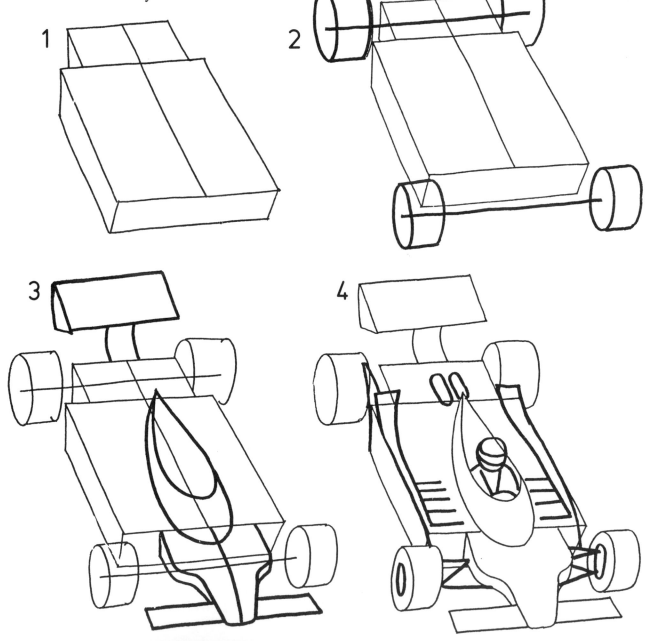

Look how smooth the wheels are compared with those on the giant dump truck on page 133. Why do you think there is such a difference?

Turbo-charged sports car

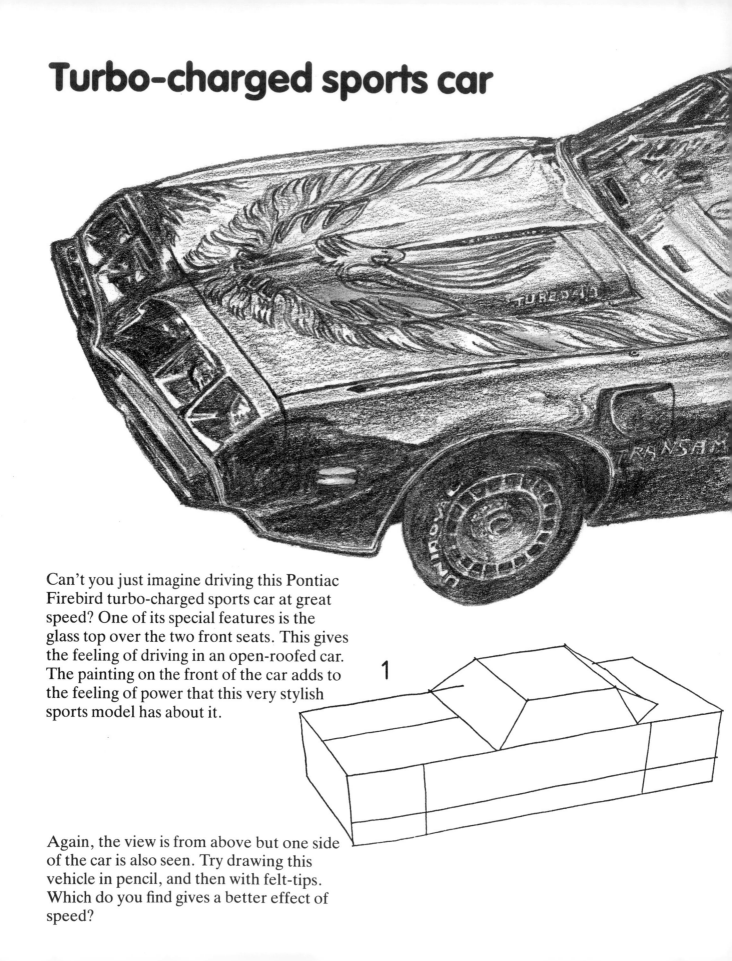

Can't you just imagine driving this Pontiac Firebird turbo-charged sports car at great speed? One of its special features is the glass top over the two front seats. This gives the feeling of driving in an open-roofed car. The painting on the front of the car adds to the feeling of power that this very stylish sports model has about it.

1

Again, the view is from above but one side of the car is also seen. Try drawing this vehicle in pencil, and then with felt-tips. Which do you find gives a better effect of speed?

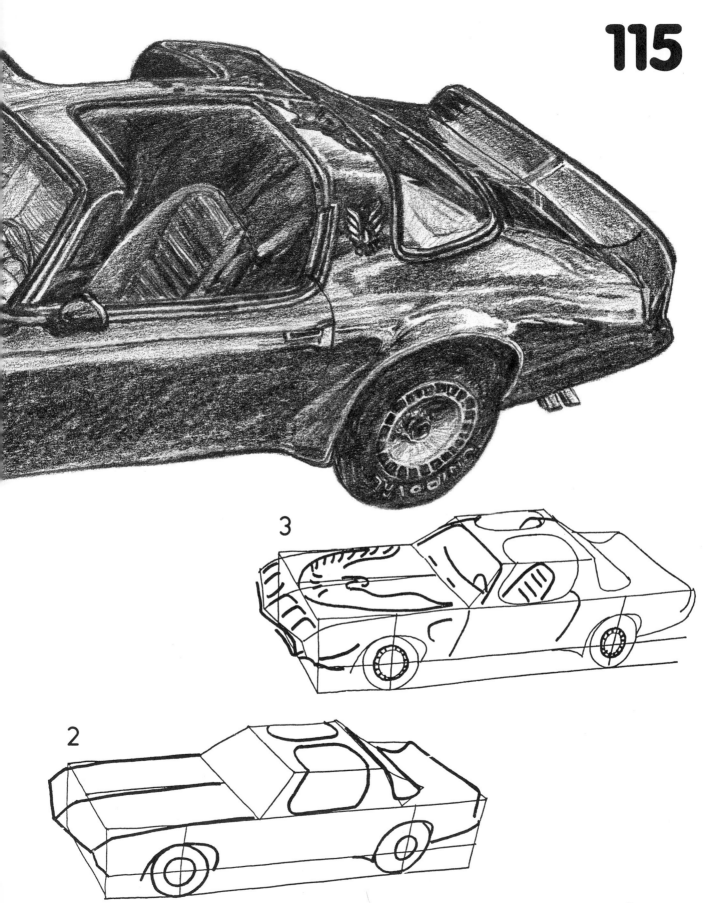

115

3

2

Perspective

Perspective helps you draw objects that seem so real that they almost come out of the page.

It is really quite easy to achieve this if you remember three important rules.

The first is that those parts of the vehicle you are drawing that are nearest to you will always look bigger, and so you must draw them bigger than the parts farther away.

The second rule is that lines and shapes seem to get closer together the farther away they are.

The third rule is that parts that are really the same size, like wheels, always look smaller if they are farther away.

Here are seven drawings, all chosen to show you what is meant by perspective. Look at each of them in turn. Notice how wheels that are farther away are always drawn smaller than those that are nearer to you.

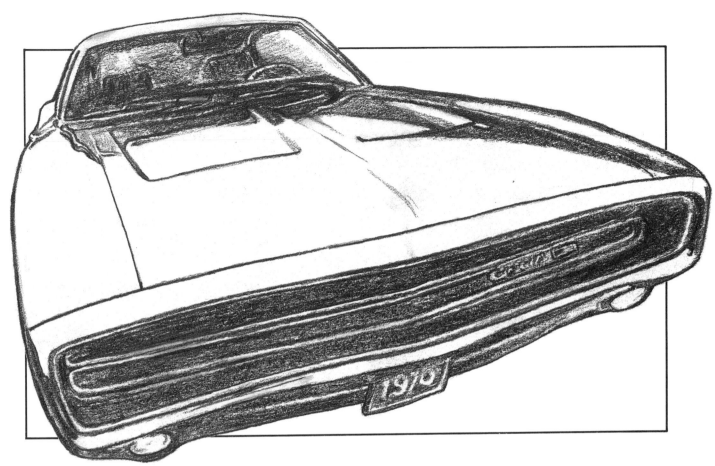

Here is a car which seems to have a wide front. But at the bottom of page 121 there is a drawing of the same car which seems to have a wider rear. This is because, in that view of the car, its rear is nearer to you.

© DIAGRAM

Custom-built Cadillac

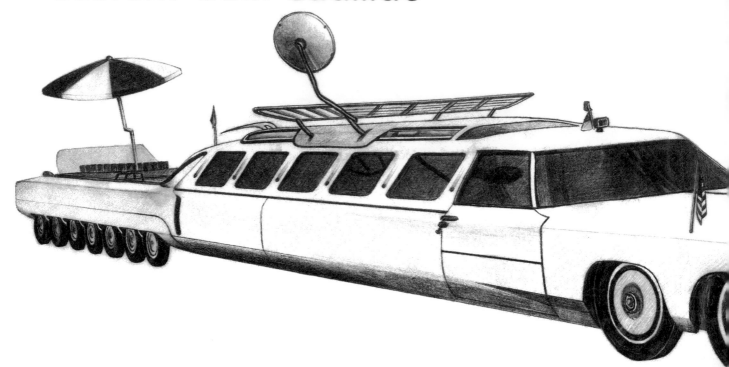

The drawing here by Brian is of a car with twenty-two wheels. It is an amazingly long vehicle. Unless you stood a good distance from it, you would not be able to include all the wheels in one drawing.

It is a custom-built Cadillac – which means it was built especially for its owner – and is 20m (67 feet) long. It has room for 50 passengers, a cinema, a TV lounge, cocktail bar, small swimming pool and sun patio.

How long is your family car? And how many of the same length do you think would fit alongside this one?

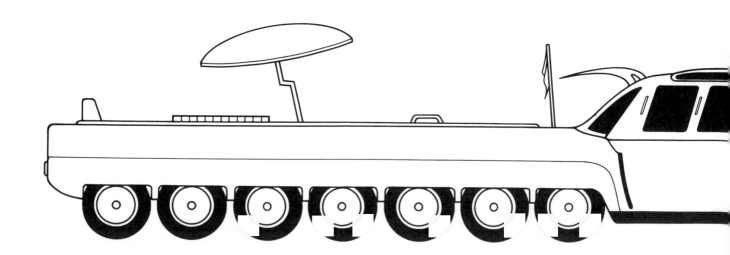

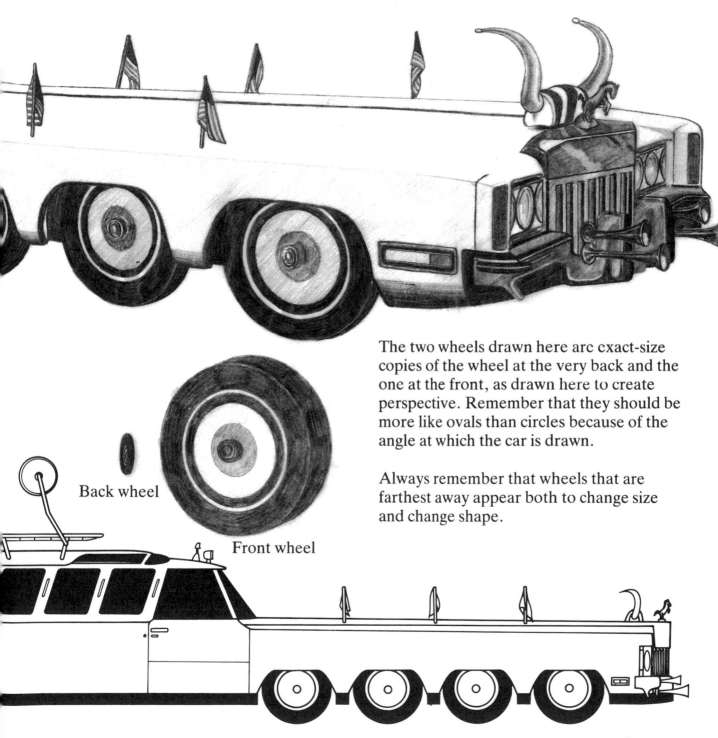

Back wheel

Front wheel

The two wheels drawn here are exact-size copies of the wheel at the very back and the one at the front, as drawn here to create perspective. Remember that they should be more like ovals than circles because of the angle at which the car is drawn.

Always remember that wheels that are farthest away appear both to change size and change shape.

Dodge Charger

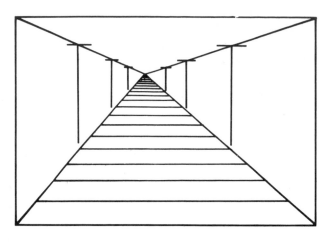

We all know that rail tracks are the same width apart all the way along the line, and that telegraph poles are the same height. But perspective makes distant objects appear smaller, and nearer objects appear larger.

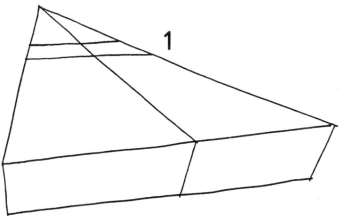

1

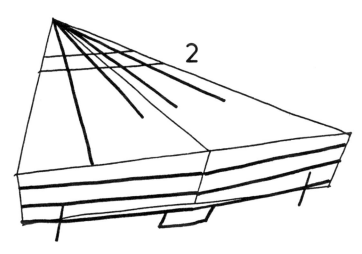

2

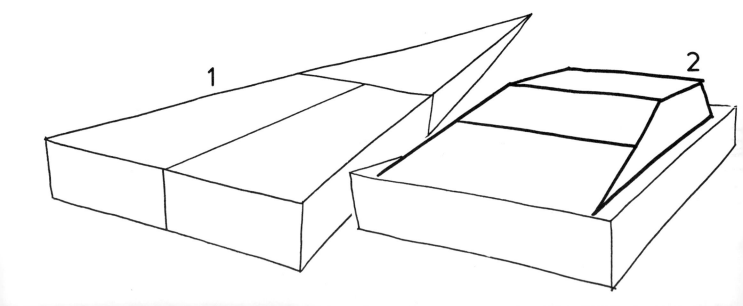

1

2

Almost all cars are the same width at the front as they are at the back. But this 1970s Dodge Charger looks as if it has an enormously wide front because it is drawn to look as if it is coming straight out of the page toward you. This is another example of the use of perspective to make objects look more real.

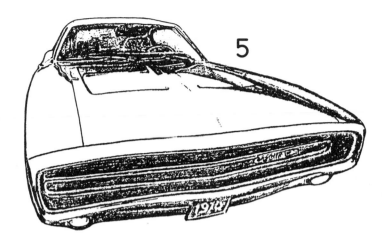

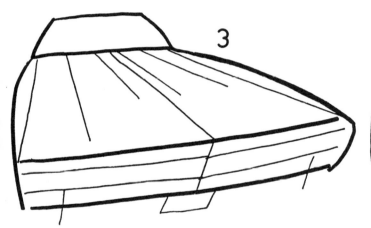

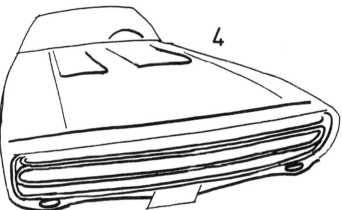

From the back, this Charger looks as if it has a very large rear bumper because this is nearer to you.

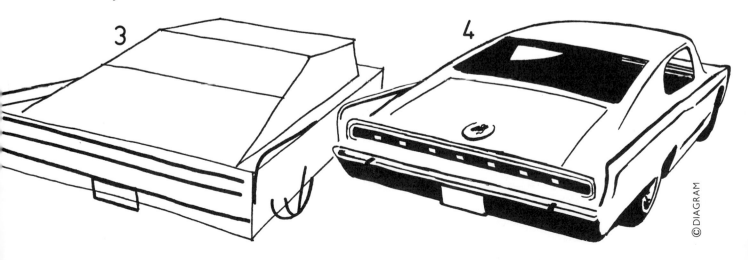

©DIAGRAM

More about perspective

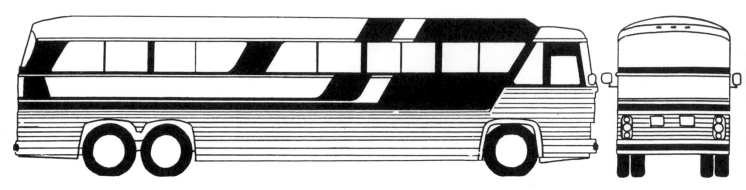

Both the vehicles on these two pages have lines going down the side as part of their decoration.

The simple side view of the bus, shown above, illustrates that the front is the same height as the back, and also that the wheels are, of course, the same size. But if you look at the drawing below, which is from an angle, you can see how, with perspective, the sides seem to get smaller the farther away they are, and so do the wheels. The same is true of the vehicle opposite. Tracing these drawings will help you to understand how sizes seem to change with distance.

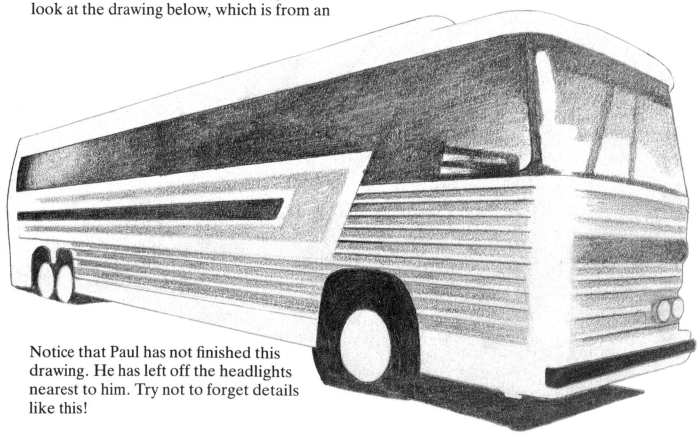

Notice that Paul has not finished this drawing. He has left off the headlights nearest to him. Try not to forget details like this!

Long-distance bus

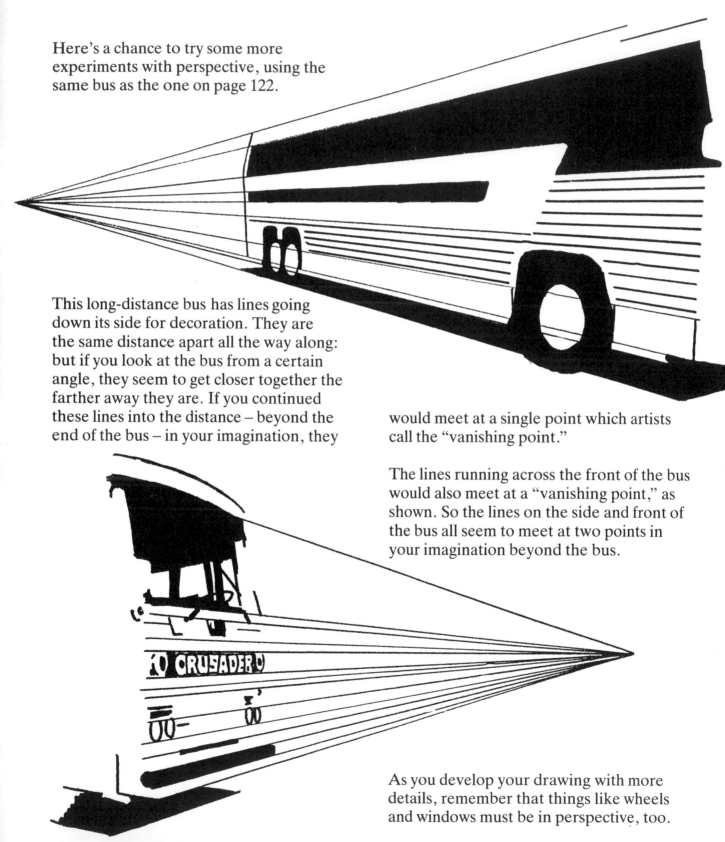

Here's a chance to try some more experiments with perspective, using the same bus as the one on page 122.

This long-distance bus has lines going down its side for decoration. They are the same distance apart all the way along: but if you look at the bus from a certain angle, they seem to get closer together the farther away they are. If you continued these lines into the distance – beyond the end of the bus – in your imagination, they would meet at a single point which artists call the "vanishing point."

The lines running across the front of the bus would also meet at a "vanishing point," as shown. So the lines on the side and front of the bus all seem to meet at two points in your imagination beyond the bus.

As you develop your drawing with more details, remember that things like wheels and windows must be in perspective, too.

CRUSADER

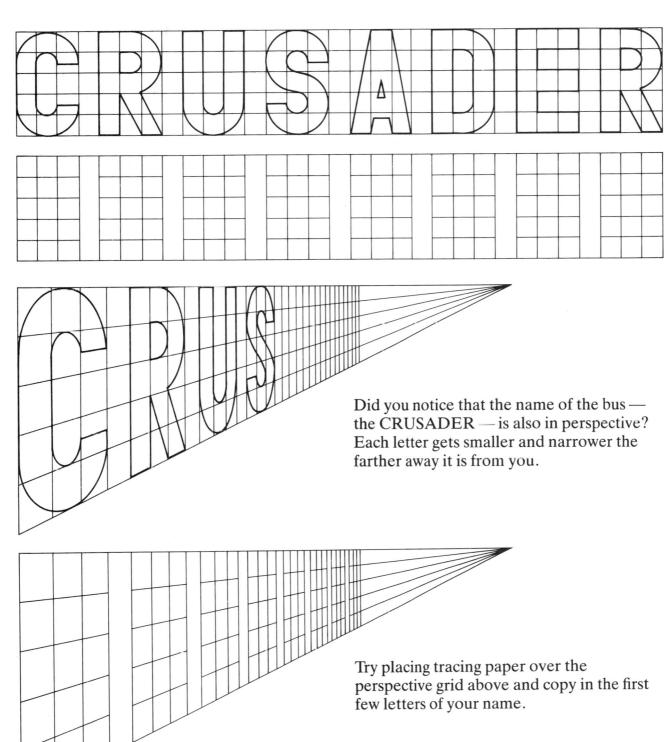

Did you notice that the name of the bus —
the CRUSADER — is also in perspective?
Each letter gets smaller and narrower the
farther away it is from you.

Try placing tracing paper over the
perspective grid above and copy in the first
few letters of your name.

©DIAGRAM

Trailer

Peter copied this vehicle from a photograph in an advertisement in a newspaper.
But, of course, the original photograph did not have his imaginary pencil lines in it to help him get the perspective right. His lines show how parts of the vehicle seem larger because they are nearer to you. Using a ruler will help you draw these imaginary lines, which you can rub out later.

These lines would all meet if only the page were much wider.

Camper

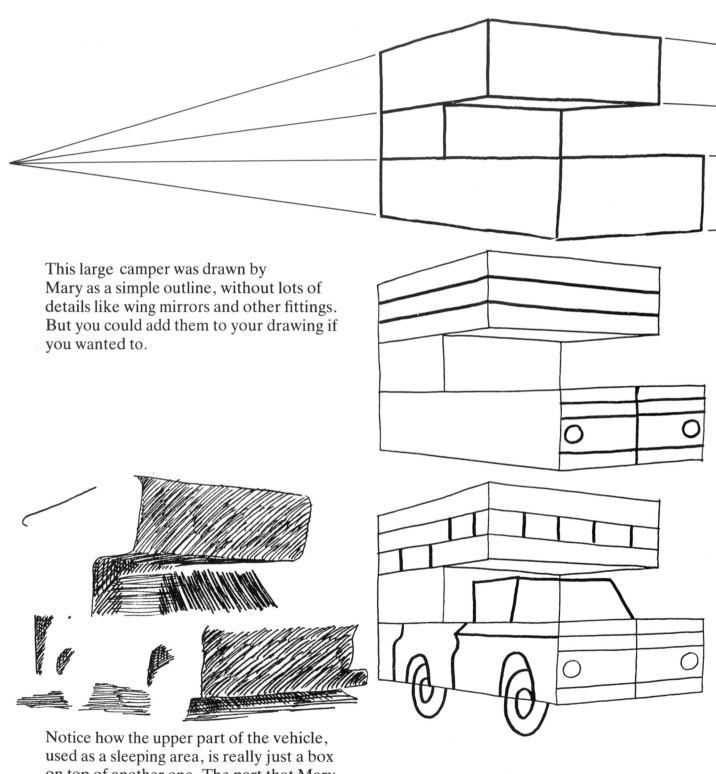

This large camper was drawn by
Mary as a simple outline, without lots of
details like wing mirrors and other fittings.
But you could add them to your drawing if
you wanted to.

Notice how the upper part of the vehicle,
used as a sleeping area, is really just a box
on top of another one. The part that Mary
has kept white and not shaded in is where
the light falls.

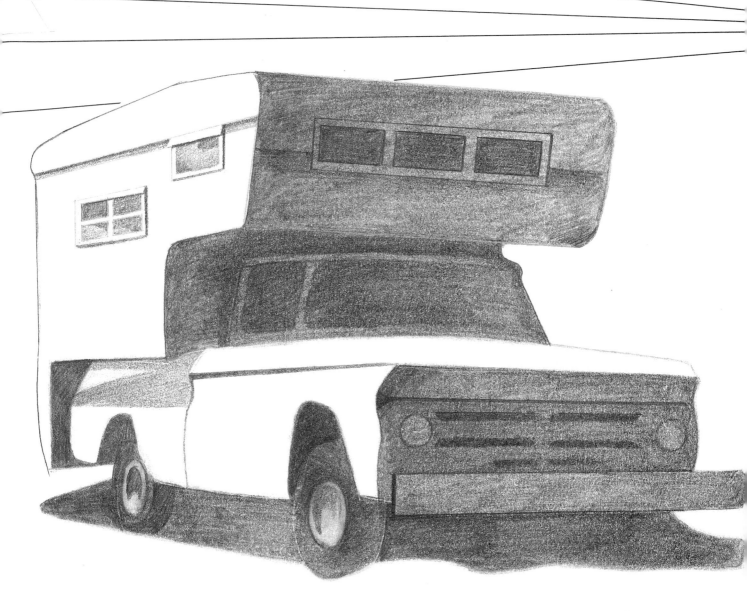

Again, the wheels at the back look smaller than those at the front because they are farther away from you.

If you have some model cars or other vehicles, place them in this sort of angle and try to draw them in perspective, sometimes from the front and sometimes from the back, as if the vehicle is moving away from you. When do the back wheels seem larger?

©DIAGRAM

Model T Ford

This is another view of the Model T Ford on pages 76–77. Because the car is at an angle, in order to get the perspective right we have to draw the wheels to look like ovals rather than circles, as shown.

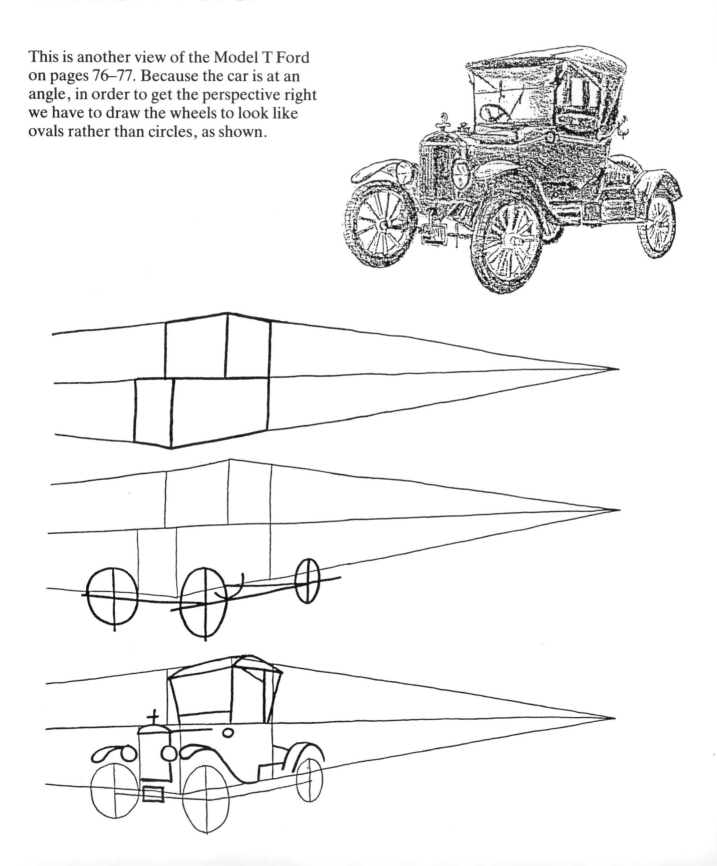

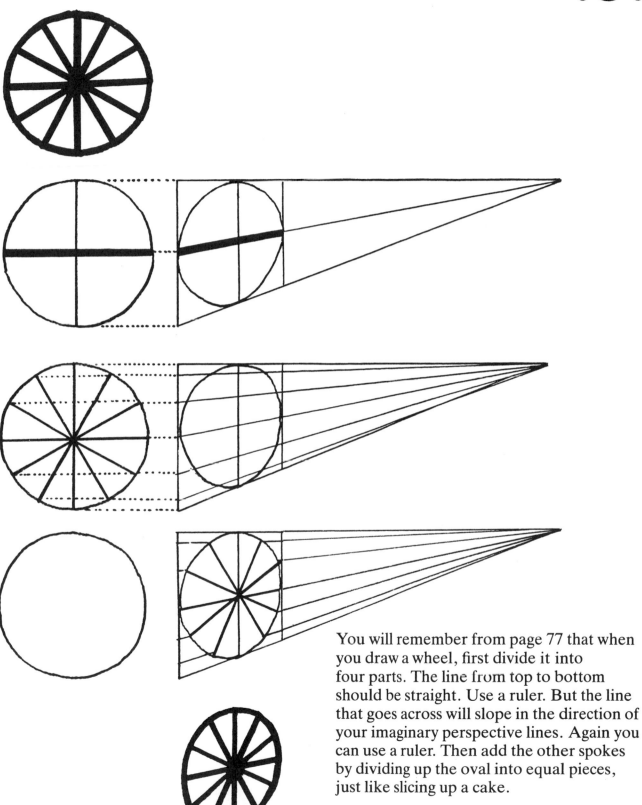

You will remember from page 77 that when you draw a wheel, first divide it into four parts. The line from top to bottom should be straight. Use a ruler. But the line that goes across will slope in the direction of your imaginary perspective lines. Again you can use a ruler. Then add the other spokes by dividing up the oval into equal pieces, just like slicing up a cake.

©DIAGRAM

Giant dump truck

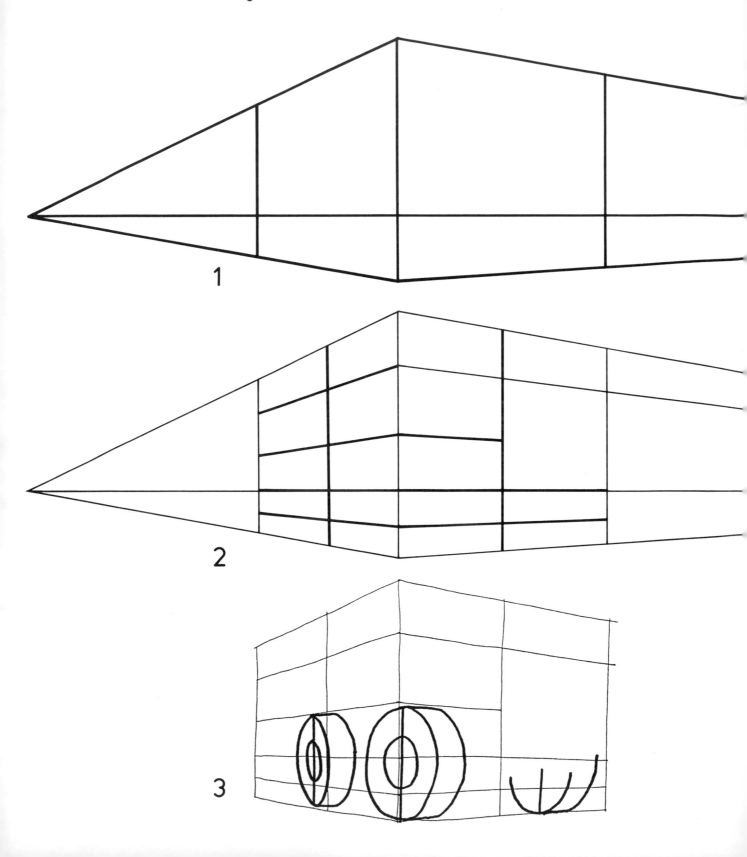

If you want to draw the dump truck in perspective, you will need extra space on your paper to draw the imaginary vanishing points.

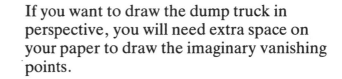

When you start this picture, remember first to draw in some perspective lines as shown here. You can rub them out later if you use a soft pencil. Then try drawing the dump truck in action.

4

5

Why do you think this vehicle needs such large wheels? They are bigger than you are! The driver's cabin is also very high up, so he needs a ladder to reach it.

©DIAGRAM

Lunar vehicle

This is an extraterrestrial vehicle, especially designed for use on the Moon.

It can climb up steep slopes and runs on two 36-volt batteries. Most family cars can carry half their own weight, but the lunar vehicle is capable of bearing up to twice its weight. Baggage is stored under the two seats; there are sample collection bags at the back, and cameras at the front, as well as radio controls for contact with base.

1

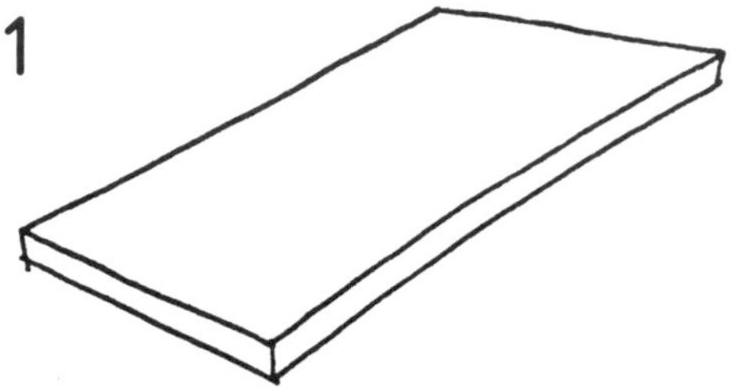

2

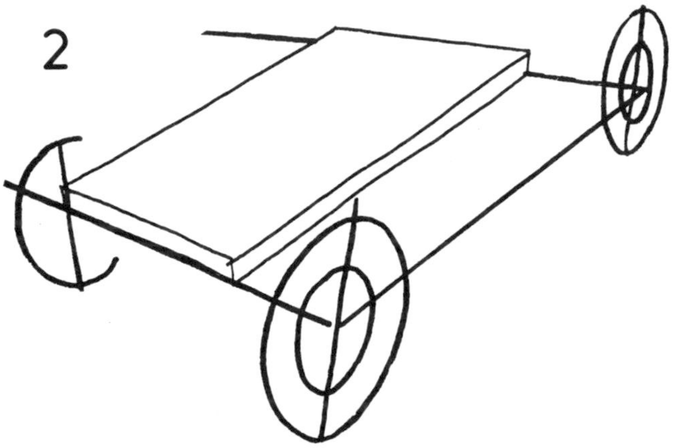

3

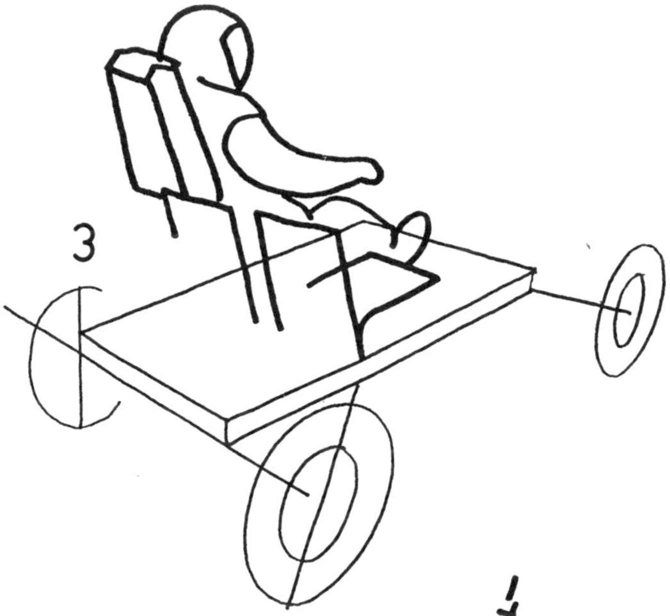

4

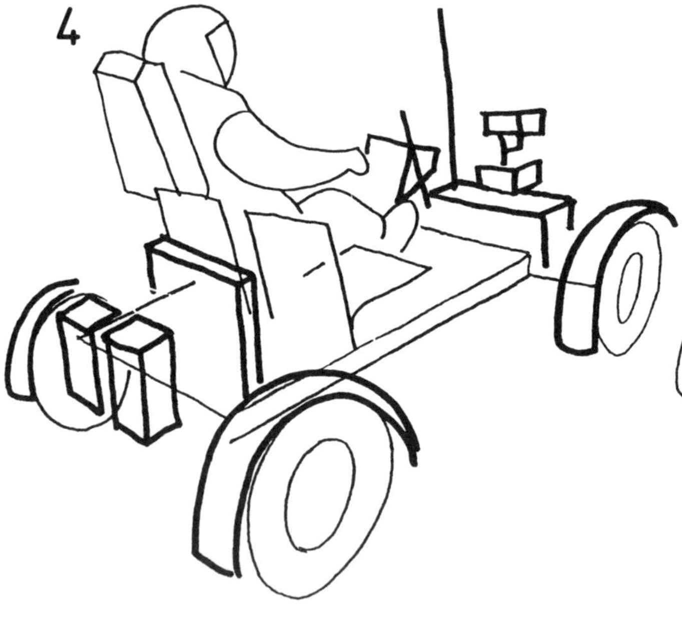

5

Graham first drew the picture in pencil but then used a brush and ink to paint in the darker areas, leaving lots of parts white. It's fun to put the driver in a spacesuit, too. You could also use the step-by-step sketches to help you draw a beach buggy.

When you copy this picture, try to think of it as just as a table on wheels.

©DIAGRAM

Fantasy cars

Now it's time to use your own imagination and design cars of the future, just as Mary has done here. The larger drawing is her idea of a jet-propelled racing car with heavy-duty wheels for rough ground. The smaller drawing is more streamlined for city use.

Try your hand at some of the following – a car that can fly to jump ahead when in a traffic jam; a car that could also run on tracks like a train; an inflatable vehicle; a mobile shop; a bicycle with four wheels; a car that can also cross water . . . and all your own inventions, too. Get going now!

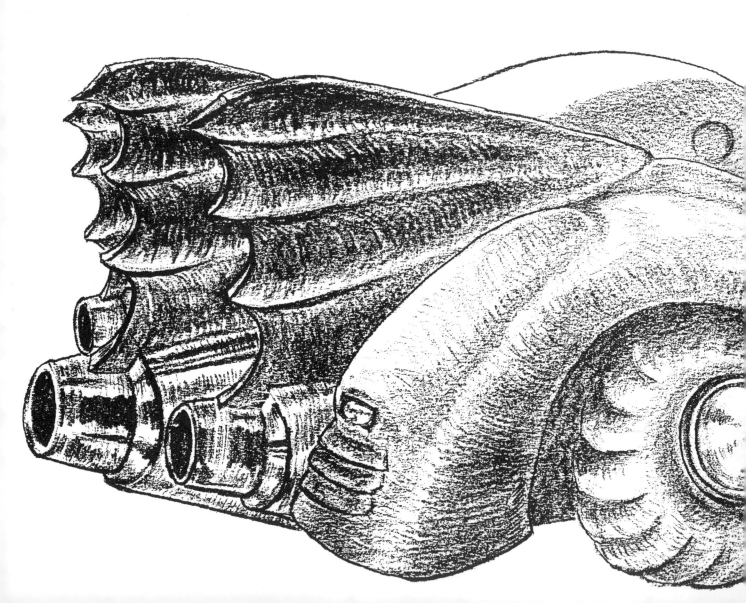

Motor maze

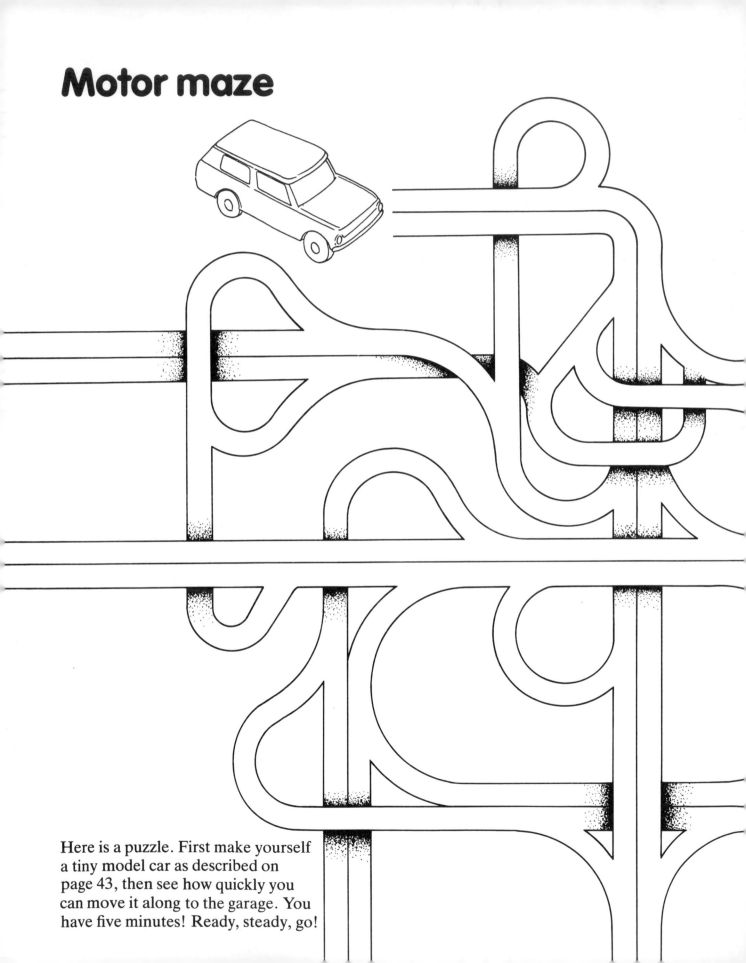

Here is a puzzle. First make yourself a tiny model car as described on page 43, then see how quickly you can move it along to the garage. You have five minutes! Ready, steady, go!

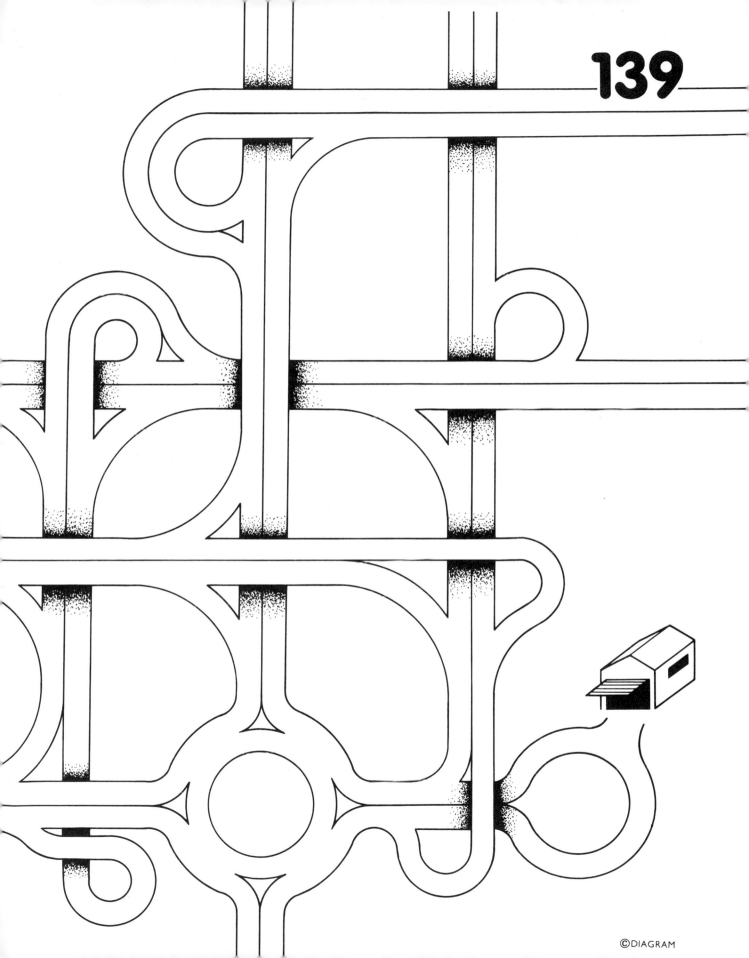

These squares can
be used for enlarging
your drawings as
shown on pages 38–39.

Index